Take control of your life

Take control
of your life

The five-step plan
to health and happiness

Dr Gail Ratcliffe

EXISLE
PUBLISHING

This edition published in 2003 in New Zealand by
Exisle Publishing Limited,
P.O. Box 60-490, Titirangi, Auckland 1230.

The original edition of *Take Control of Your Life* first published in Australia and
New Zealand by Simon & Schuster Australia in 1995.

ISBN 978-0-908988-30-3

Reprinted 2009

Text design and production by *Book*NZ (www.booknz.co.nz)
Cover design by Richard Wheatley (Red Design)
Printed in China through Colorcraft Ltd., Hong Kong

www.exislepublishing.com

Contents

Introduction

They are not long the weeping and the laughter
Love, desire and hate:
I think they have no portion in us after
We pass the gate.

LORENZO DOW

Life is not an introductory offer. From the day you are born, you're paying full price. Since every human being is *guaranteed* only one life, you'd think we would spend a lot of time ensuring that our stay on this earth was free of regret and turmoil, but circumstances conspire to prevent this for the vast majority of people.

It's a stress-filled world

The 1990s were known as the age of anxiety. It is predicted that the first decade of the third millennium will be known as the age of depression. The proportion of people who now suffer depression or anxiety of clinical severity is one in five, and a World Bank Report to the United Nations predicts that depression will go from the fourth ranked cause of disability and death to the second by 2020. Today, there has never seemed more need for control and certainty. We have endured a decade of wars, economic crises and environmental disasters and the new century has changed little. Conflict and political instability still surround us in Europe, the African continent, the

Middle East and Asia, and more countries are nuclear capable than 10 years ago. Even if your country is untouched by these conflicts, can you be certain that globalisation will not threaten your job security or that you will not suffer stress or burnout or depression because of the conditions you work under? Can you be sure how continued climate changes, the Greenhouse effect, and the ongoing pollution of land, water and food will affect you and your children by the end of the decade?

These concerns and others form an ominous undertone to the tenor of everyday life. They both create and magnify the existing stresses of day-to-day living. They can make you feel powerless, and they can cause you to despair, to cease trying and to become helpless.

In addition, there are new and more insidious forms of stress than there were 10 years ago. The technology that allows you to keep in touch with distant family members and friends, to find information fast, and to make friends with people on the other side of the world is also replacing normal human interactions. Many people are living 'virtual lives', interfacing with their computer rather than with real people. A study in the *American Psychologist* reports that the more time you spend on the Internet, the more likely it is that your social supports will crumble and the more you are vulnerable to unhappiness, depression and loneliness.

Technology is also helping to speed up the world and to overload you with information. With laptops you can work anywhere, anytime. With email, mobile phones and pagers you can be contacted anywhere, anytime. Time becomes a scarce commodity and the balance departs from your life as you work longer hours and more days of the week.

The results of a recent study show that the annual US medical bill for stress tops $400 billion and that anxiety disorders now cost the US economy almost $42 billion a year. In most Western countries suicides have increased, particularly among teenagers, and stress and depression are seen at increasingly younger ages. Ten years ago it was not uncommon for children of eight and nine to be treated for stress. Now we recognise depression in preschoolers and suicide is the sixth leading cause of death for 5–14-year-olds.

The rates of depression and anxiety are increasing, and these problems are occurring at earlier ages.

Where are the solutions?

In times of uncertainty like these, people search for solutions. The search extends to religion and astrology, tarot cards and numerology, courses and counselling, textbooks and tapes, to fix up lives that are damaged or unsatisfying.

You can learn to control your life and produce the outcomes you want. You can learn how to be contented and happy, and confident that you know how to remain this way through good times and bad. But it won't come through magic or easy fixes. It certainly won't come through anything that relies exclusively on external forces: luck, fate or other people. Taking charge of your life requires self-knowledge, a belief in your self-efficacy (how you judge the skills and abilities you have) and acquiring some basic skills of self-change. It means understanding what it takes to make your life balanced and satisfying.

> *You can learn to control your life and produce the outcomes you want. This requires self-knowledge, belief in your abilities and learning how to change.*

The Five Step Life Plan

This book is based on a method of life planning and stress management that has been developed and refined in clinical practice for over 13 years: the Five Step Life Plan. This plan reflects current changes in the focus of psychology. These changes incorporate both the concept of positive psychology and the integration of the social and biological approaches to understanding human behaviour. Rather than focus only on fixing what is not working well in your life, positive psychology looks at strategies for enhancing your ability to cope and for preventing mental health problems in the future. The integration of the social and biological bases of human behaviour reveals that it is not only what happens in your life, but also the way your brain and its chemicals work that affects how you see the world and whether you cope well and achieve to your maximum potential.

The Five Step Life Plan is a blueprint for taking control of your life. Not only does it deal with managing the unpleasant events in your world, but it also includes information about how to analyse what kind of a life you want, and how to achieve it.

- How to stop stress now and so prevent yourself sliding into depression.

- How to create in yourself those skills, attitudes and behaviours that will prevent stress in the future.
- How to achieve the goals you set.
- How to develop the expertise to create the life you personally desire, whatever form that may take.

> *The Five Step Life Plan is a blueprint for taking control of your life. It offers strategies for helping you cope with, or prevent, anxiety and depression.*

Mind controlling the body

This book also offers you an up-to-date insight into the chemical bases of happiness. Achieving happiness has been the object of our desires for centuries. Through the ages philosophers and writers have supplied us with insights and intuitions which spring from their examinations of this elusive state.

We stand now at the frontiers of investigation into the biochemical bases of moods. Research into the chemicals that cause moods to change from neutral or negative into positive suggests that there are universal 'uppers'. These include activities like sex and being in love, massage, exercise, laughter and being in the sunlight. We now know that your life will be happier and more fulfilling if you balance it with these and with other activities that shut off the stress cycle. We also know that these activities will help you live longer. The new disciplines of cognitive neuroscience and psycho-neuroimmunology explore the mechanisms whereby mental activity regulates the body. The impact of our emotions on our physical health is called MindBody medicine.

> *Activities that improve your mood also enhance your immune system and prolong your life.*

The methods you will learn in this book work with people of all ages. The Five Step Life Plan has been taught to children as young as nine or 10. Its principles are clear and straightforward and easy to understand. It works with people of all levels of intelligence and all socioeconomic backgrounds. It has been taught to university professors and students, and it has been taught to prisoners in jail who cannot read or write. It has been taught to business people and politicians and to disadvantaged youth.

What will you learn?

Self-analysis

The first part of the book, Chapters 1–3, is devoted to self-analysis:

- Ways to recognise what is wrong with your life and pinpoint why it feels out of control.
- How to identify the stress you experience when your life is slipping from your grasp, to find out what is causing it, and understand all the effects it has on you.

Planning your life

The second part of the book, Chapters 4–9, covers the way you can plan the life that you want to live.

- How you can eliminate your stress or manage it.
- How to decide what you will put into your life that will balance and enhance it.

At the end of each of Chapters 5–9 is a section that outlines how to design your own individually tailored Life Plan – a plan that identifies and minimises your stress and that recognises and maximises your enjoyments and your opportunities to reach your goals.

The book, as a whole, includes comments and case studies from people who have used the Five Step Life Plan, and some of the strategies they have selected to construct the lives they want to live.

> By the end of this book you will have the self-understanding and the ability to help direct your life according to your wishes.

What kind of life do you want?

What do you need to create a satisfying experience? One essential requirement is to have thought about the kind of life you want to live. Is life simply to be endured or is it a dynamic, invigorating experience?

> *You need to think about the kind of life you want.*

Conditioning holds you back

> *I was talking to my mother about what she intended to do with herself now that my father has died and she said, 'I suppose I ought to make some plans – I've never thought about that sort of thing before. My generation didn't really think about what kind of life they wanted to lead, they just accepted what came along. I suppose we did what everyone else did without questioning it.' I thought, 'It's not just your generation, it's most people.'*

You come to value conformity through the process of learning to be 'human'. Your parents present you with early models of adult behaviour: 'Hold your knife like this ... This is the way you tie your shoe laces ... I'll show you how to ride a bike.' This pattern of imitation is continued by your teachers at school and your friends. You develop the belief that to conform to the behaviour of others is good and not to conform is bad.

> *You are programmed to accept a version of life without examining whether it is the version you actually want.*

The specific messages you receive throughout the course of your life encourage you to conform. They prevent you from thinking in an original way.
    Some of these messages originate way back in childhood:

* 'What will the neighbours think?'
* 'Nice girls/boys don't do that.'
* 'Work hard at school, get a good job and you'll be happy and successful.'
* 'Find the right partner, get married and live happily ever after.'

Some of our expectations about success and happiness are sure to be dashed, however. It is predicted that the average school leaver of today will have to retrain for an entirely new career three times before retiring. Marriages aren't forever: 40 percent of all adults now are single. The percentage is the same in most Western countries, and it is rising. Most people getting married today will spend a major part of their adult life as a single person.

The conditioning you receive through your education, your religion and your culture (via your parents, teachers and friends, and even through the media) does not equip you to examine your life closely. Living an unexamined life is not usually a recipe for happiness. You need to be able to see yourself clearly in order to make changes when things go wrong or to create a fulfilling life.

Because of your early programming, you are more likely to adapt to circumstances when you don't feel you match up to what is expected of you than you are to change them. Inevitably you end up feeling vaguely dissatisfied and short-changed by the world.

At 25 I thought my life was over. I was married with two children, I wasn't working, I'd given up university when I got pregnant, my husband treated me like a slave. I was bored and depressed, and I accepted it. I thought, 'There isn't any gold at the end of the rainbow; life's basically just a kick in the face.'

> **You need to be able to see yourself clearly in order to make changes when things go wrong and to lead a fulfilling life.**

Breaking free

In order to break free of your conditioning, to take control of your life and be happy, you need to be able to do two things.

Find and fix what is wrong

First, and most importantly, in order to create the world you want, you need to be able to analyse and fix what is wrong with your present existence. Being able to put right the things that are wrong in your life is essential to living it the way you want to.

- What are the barriers that prevent you from creating a fulfilling existence?
- How do your past programming and experience affect the way you presently run your life?

- What should you do to resolve the problems of today and make sure tomorrow runs smoothly?

These questions are answered in this book.

Live the life you really want

The second is to stop living an unexamined life, and accepting an existence that you feel is substandard. Consider how often you ask yourself questions like these:

- Am I the person I want to be?
- What makes me happy?
- What are my goals in life?
- Am I living the kind of life I want to live?

By the end of this book you will have provided your own answers to these questions.

You may be aware that your world is not entirely as you would choose it to be. Many people come to a point when suddenly everything seems out of control. For others it is not a sudden realisation; they may never have felt they had a good enough grip on life.

> *Being able to put right the things that are wrong in your life is essential to living it the way you want to.*

The desire to control your world

A survey commissioned by a major newspaper in the southern hemisphere in 1993 attempted to construct a record of the average citizen's attitudes, hopes, dreams, loves and hates. In most replies, the emotional strength of the family overwhelmed everything else as a major source of values, but in the section that asked participants to rate what they considered to be indicators of success, 88 percent judged 'Being in control of my own life' as the top indicator. 'Having a good marriage or relationship with my partner' came in second at 82 percent and 'Having children I can be proud of' came third with 77 percent.

The desire to control your world and to be able to predict to some extent your future is a basic human need. If you alter babies' schedules – bath them at a different time of day, for example – they'll often get fussy and upset. Children a little older crave predictability too. There comes an age at which they refuse to go down in any bed but their own or in any room but their own. Try to make them and they won't sleep, or they'll wake crying half a dozen times a night. In the animal world there is evidence that controlling rewards is more desirable than getting them for nothing. Research shows that both pigeons and rats prefer to push a lever to obtain their food (as long as the task is not too difficult) than have it freely given.

> Wanting to control your world is a basic human need.
> You want to be able to direct or improve your life,
> to set your goals and to achieve them.

Of course, control has negative connotations too: brainwashing and hypnosis are types of control you might want to resist. But these are forms of influence by others rather than versions of self-control. The verb 'control' has two meanings. One is 'to curb or hold back', the other is 'to have charge of, to direct'. What is meant in this book by control is the latter: the ability to direct or enhance your life, to set your goals and to achieve them.

In fact, control and freedom are closely allied. Freedom can be seen as an ability:

> *There are two sides of freedom: freedom from (independence)*
> *and freedom to (ability, performance).*
>
> NIETZSCHE

Internal and external control

Self-control or control of one's own world is one of the predominant themes running through the psychological literature since the late 1950s. Many psychologists have argued that people have a basic motivation to gain a sense of mastery over their environments. In 1966 Julian Rotter suggested that there was a distinction between people who believed that control of their world was in their own hands and those who believe that control lies in external forces – luck, fate or other people. He said the first group have an internal locus of control (locus means place or area). The second group have an external locus of control.

> *Having internal control means believing that control of your world is in your own hands.*

You can see that the second group, those who believe they are subject to external forces, are really operating in terms of the first definition of control, 'to curb or hold back', whereas those who have an internal locus of control operate according to the second definition. They believe they 'have charge of, or direct' their own lives.

According to Rotter's research, people who believe they can control their own lives will do so. People who believe they cannot control their lives are more easily pressured and manipulated by others, they persevere less and they even cope with disasters differently. When recuperating from heart attacks, individuals with an external locus of control are more passive and less co-operative with their nurses. Externals are also more likely to give up and walk away after a major disaster like a flood, whereas people with an internal locus of control are more likely to start rebuilding.

> *Those who believe they can control their own lives will do so.*

Self-efficacy

A decade after Rotter, Albert Bandura developed his theory of self-efficacy. Your belief in your self-efficacy is your personal judgement about your ability to cope with or take charge of your life – efficacy means effectiveness, having the power to produce the effect you want. Your perceived self-efficacy relates not to the actual capabilities you have, but to the way you judge whatever skills you have. According to Bandura's theory, when you are confronted with a potentially stressful situation, your self-efficacy belief affects your reaction to the situation. If you believe you can cope with or change it, you are more likely to, and you are less likely to be emotionally upset while you do so.

Bandura's studies supported his theory that people who believe they can cope will do so. Later research showed that this effectiveness extends over a wide variety of areas. You'll look after your health better and you'll survive the deaths of those close to you with more resilience if your self-efficacy is high. For example, studies showed that you are more able to give up smoking if you have high self-efficacy than if you don't. You're even more likely to practise safe sex!

Researchers interviewing people who lost family in the volcanic eruption of Mt St Helens in the United States reported that people who had high self-efficacy were better able to cope with their loss. Those with low self-efficacy were still feeling depressed and showing the physical symptoms of stress three years later.

> *Efficacy means having the power to produce the effect you want. And if you believe you can cope with or change a situation, you are more likely to do so.*

Getting self-efficacy

How do you get high self-efficacy? You get it by taking control of your life. That sounds a bit of a catch-22, doesn't it? If your self-efficacy is low, that's the last thing you'll do. But, more recent research by Bandura has shown that if you know how to take charge of your life and you do it in manageable steps, you can increase your self-efficacy and go on to achieve goals you thought were totally out of your reach. You can even extend your life.

> *If you know how to take charge of your life, you can increase your self-efficacy.*

A landmark study in an old people's home suggested that exerting even a little more control over the events in your life will contribute to you living longer. All the residents in the home were given a plant. Half were told that they alone were responsible for watering and feeding their plant. The other half had theirs cared for by nursing home staff. All the residents were frail and ill; the only difference between them was whether they cared for their own plant or not. The group who cared for their own plants lived longer.

Evidence like this sufficiently convinced a joint task force of the American Medical and Nursing Associations to conclude that 'a sense of purpose and control over one's life is integral to the health of the aged'. In fact, as you will see later, it is integral to your health – physical and mental – at all ages.

> *A sense of purpose and control over your life is vital to physical and mental health, at all ages.*

What happens when you don't control your life?

Research has shown that if you believe you don't have control over the upsetting events in your life, you are more likely to develop depression. A study of high school teachers in urban Los Angeles found that most of them experienced severe job-related stress. Seventy-six percent said their stress was moderate to severe, and 20 percent said it was almost unbearable. Not all of them became depressed, though. Those who did were teachers who believed that neither they nor anyone else could control the stresses under which they worked.

When you continually fail to take control of events in your life, or you are unable to, depression is not the only result. You can become so helpless that even when circumstances change, and you are able to take control, you won't try.

Learned helplessness and depression

Original research on learned helplessness began in the 1960s with animals, and continued later with human subjects. The behaviour of both adults and children was observed in relation to academic learning and problem-solving. The results showed that when people were not able to control the situation in which they were supposed to perform, not only did they give up trying but they became incapable of learning or thinking clearly, and they were more likely to become anxious and frightened.

Martin Seligman, who conducted much of the early research, has gone on to demonstrate that learned helplessness can manifest itself in pessimism, resignation, childhood failures, fear of decision-making, loss of motivation and, in extreme cases, sudden death. Seligman says that the emotional distresses that lead to depression, anxiety and failure do not simply happen; they 'grow out of a sense of helplessness that is learned, reinforced and justified by the individual'. Current thinking on depression suggests that a loss of control over your life causes helplessness, which in turn makes you depressed.

Loss of control over your life can cause helplessness,
which in turn makes you depressed.

Optimism overcomes helplessness

In line with the focus on positive psychology, Seligman and other researchers are now investigating 'optimism', the expectation that good things will happen, as an antidote to learned helplessness. Although they don't agree on the exact definition of optimism, they do accept that it can be learned and that optimists and pessimists cope differently with stress. We will look into this in more detail later, but in general, optimists persevere more in life than pessimists, they stick at things and they solve their problems. They also report themselves more satisfied with the quality of their lives than pessimists. You can see that being an optimist is similar to having a high level of perceived self-efficacy, and like Bandura's theory, control is the crucial factor. Seligman suggests that the perception that your own actions controlled the experience can help produce self-esteem and a sense of competence as well as protecting against depression.

Optimism can help cope with stress and overcome learned
helplessness. And optimism can be learned.

Being out of control of your life for a period of time can affect you profoundly, not just at the time, but later too. We will see the extent of this more clearly in later chapters of this book, in the histories of people who have been through traumatic childhoods – the victims of physical, sexual or emotional abuse.

The evidence is compelling. The more you take charge of your life, the more likely you are to reach your goals, the more you will believe in yourself, the less stressed and depressed you will be, and the more you will continue to control your own destiny.

The more you take charge of your life, the more likely you are to
reach your goals, believe in yourself, cope with stress, and
continue to control your own destiny.

What this book will do for you

This book will give you the concrete advice that will allow you to take control of your own life. It is a book different to most others on the market. It is not one that describes your problems but offers you no advice on how to change them. Nor is it a New Age human potential, 'you can have anything you want, if you'll only be positive' book. It won't tell you that you will 'achieve unprecedented excellence', 'unleash unlimited power' and 'become wealthy and successful'. Such promises are unrealistic. Such books generally promise more than they can deliver: you may not have hidden depths; you may not have a passion to succeed at all costs; you may not want fame and fortune. Also, life is more complex than this. One technique on its own cannot possibly be the answer to all the problems faced by everyone in the world.

Such 'easy fix' books tend to be single-solution oriented. The solution may be positive thinking, it may be making affirmations, it may be believing in yourself, which are all useful techniques – some of which are discussed later in this book – but whatever the magic formula is, there is always a major ingredient missing. That ingredient is knowing how to understand and deal with the helplessness and stress caused by being out of control. Once you know how to do this, you can get your life on track again. Rotter, Bandura and Seligman's research consistently shows that stress occurs when your life is out of control and that it is stress which prevents you from regaining control. Whichever comes first, stress or feeling out of control, if you know how to deal with stress, you can then begin to run your life properly.

> *This book helps you understand and deal with the helplessness and stress caused by being out of control. If you know how to deal with stress, you can then begin to run your life properly.*

Stress can poison your peace of mind and wreck your physical wellbeing. It provides you with an endless parade of physical problems from headaches to heart attacks, it takes away your confidence and can trigger phobias, depression and mental disorders. It puts blinders on you; it changes your personality, predisposing you to react in ways that will make you even more unhappy. A common example of the way stress produces more problems is the use of drugs and alcohol to deal with fears and anxieties. Keep on taking these without addressing your real problems and before long they will have you spinning even further out of control.

Stress can also limit your perception of the present to the point where you see no solution to what ails you except to endure it or to control some aspect of life that is irrelevant to your problems. One of the most sinister effects of stress is the way it can paralyse your ability to make rational decisions. A commonly accepted explanation of compulsive tidiness, where you clean your house to within an inch of its life, is that you attempt to control the disorder in your house because you cannot control anything else in your life.

But this is not a traditional stress management book. Stress management textbooks generally provide you with a catalogue of techniques – time-management, relaxation, meditation, yoga, positive thinking, some of which are too complicated for you to learn from a book – from which you are expected to select those that will make you personally feel less stressed. Like the New Age books, these books also omit essential information from the catalogue. You need to understand what happens to you mentally, emotionally and physically when you're unhappy and out of control, in order for you to be able to select the techniques and solutions that are right for you. You need to be able to identify your own individual symptoms of stress and you need to know whether you have any biochemical imbalances that will make it harder for you to deal with your stress. All human beings are different. Only when you can identify how you uniquely react to being stressed can you select the particular stress reduction techniques which will work best for you, and will allow you to take control of your life again.

> *You need to understand what happens to you mentally, emotionally and physically when you're unhappy and out of control. Then you can select the right techniques and solutions.*

The worst of these books simply describe in detail one method of reducing stress – relaxation or meditation, for example – and imply that if you do this, all your problems will be solved and your life will automatically be happy and run as you want it. This is nonsense. Because of the way the human body operates, no single technique of stress reduction can possibly control your stress, as you will see in Chapter 1, far less make you happy as well.

Most importantly, though, traditional stress management books generally tend to foster a 'backs to the wall' mentality. They are at the opposite end of the spectrum from the positiveness of the New Age human potential books. They emphasise how you can survive or endure the events that make you feel unhappy, when what you want is how to control and create a life that is balanced and positive. You need to know how you can increase your own self-efficacy.

Hundreds of thousands of people buy both New Age human potential and stress management books, and yet neither approach on its own offers the essential formula: a complete and realistic recipe for taking control of your life, achieving the outcomes you want and creating an existence that is the way you want it to be.

If you follow the instructions in this book and practise the skills it teaches, you will increase your self-efficacy and the ability to take control of your world. You will discover how to create a balanced life based on peace and contentment, which embraces pleasure, challenge and achievement. You will achieve a life that does not focus on the regrets and the guilt of yesterday or the fears and anxieties of tomorrow, but a life that is lived to the full today.

To 'live in the present' is not a new concept; Horace, a Roman poet of the first century AD, said:

Happy the man and happy he alone,
Who can call today his own,
He who secure within can say,
Tomorrow do thy worst,
For I have lived today.

But today, some 20 centuries later, we know how to 'live in the present' in the best ways possible.

> *This book offers a complete and realistic recipe for taking control, achieving the outcomes you want and creating a balanced and positive life.*

Summing up

- You are guaranteed only one life.
- We all live in a world of increasing uncertainty and stress.
- You can learn to control your own happiness regardless of circumstances.
- Following the Five Step Life Plan enhances your wellbeing and shows you how to break down the barriers to a fulfilling existence.
- The Plan is based on up-to-date biochemical research on what produces happiness and prolongs your life.

Why does your life get out of control?

*One is not disturbed by things
but by the views one takes of them.*

EPICTETUS

Understanding your body

From the time you first enter this world, you act upon it. You test its limits and learn from this testing. Human beings are constantly involved in a search for meaning and mastery. But it is only by understanding fully your own essential human limitations that you can make complete sense out of your world, and formulate wise decisions about how to change it. It is the limitations of the human body, the way your body is built, that cause you to lose control of your life.

Have you ever wondered why you become irritable at home when you've had a hard day at work, or when you're worried about something? Have you ever noticed that the time you have most trouble making decisions is when you have something really important on your mind? Or that you always come down with a cold or the flu just when the pressure is on the most? Your body is a fascinating territory of delicate balances, feedback loops and catch-22s. When you are stressed, your body reacts.

Understanding the whole stress story means understanding your body. That understanding will help to free you from anger and worry. It will allow you to make your decisions wisely, to be healthier than you've ever been before, and as a result to feel calm, confident and in control of your life.

> *Understanding and dealing with stress means*
> *understanding your body.*

What is stress?

One of the earliest researchers in the field, Hans Selye, defines stress as 'the non-specific response of the body to any demand made on it'. But that is far too general and it does not explain enough about the various ways stress can affect you, or why people constantly talk about reducing stress. The fact is that your body reacts physically in a similar way to situations associated with excitement and pleasure as it does to situations which are unpleasant, but it is only when you are reacting to an unpleasant situation that you seek to reduce your stress. Even in an unpleasant situation, a certain amount of stress can be positive. A little stress is motivating; too much stress is debilitating. A certain amount of anxiety before an exam, for example, can sharpen your perceptions and make you more able to cope, to remember things you thought you had forgotten, and to help you construct a good answer. Too much stress and you go to pieces; you can remember nothing, and you write rubbish.

Figure 1 (next page) shows this relationship quite clearly: beyond a certain critical level, the more stress you have, the poorer your performance will be, whether it is physical or mental activity you are engaged in.

> *A little stress is motivating, but too much is debilitating.*
> *Beyond a certain level, the more stress you have,*
> *the poorer your performance will be.*

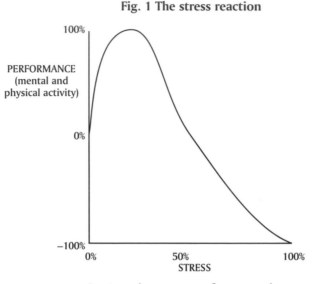

Fig. 1 The stress reaction

As stress increases performance decreases

Two conditions have to operate before you feel the need to reduce your stress:

• when it is associated with events that are perceived as unpleasant, and
• when it gets beyond that certain critical intensity.

The dictionary definition of stress as 'mental, emotional or physical strain or tension – shortened from distress' is nearer the meaning used in this book. It pertains to stress at the unpleasant end of the spectrum and to stress that is intense enough to disturb your emotional equilibrium. Stress in this book is defined as 'your reaction – mental, emotional, physical and behavioural – to any thought or event that upsets you negatively'.

> *Stress is your reaction – mental, emotional, physical and*
> *behavioural – to any thought or event that*
> *upsets you negatively.*

What happens when you get stressed?

When you are confronted with anything that is emotionally disturbing to you, certain changes occur in your body. These are known as the stress reaction, but they do not just affect your body, they affect your behaviour as well. The physical, the mental and the emotional are inextricably entwined, and all affect the way you behave.

The stress reaction can be seen as a four-stage process, involving your thoughts, your emotions, the chemical reactions in your brain and your body, and the physical sensations you feel as a result of these. But the stress reaction is not just a process that starts and then stops. Once it begins, it has a life of its own. Once you start to get upset, everything conspires to make you continue to be upset. You spin like a rat in a treadmill. Being unable to break out of that cycle sends your life spinning out of your control as well.

> *The stress reaction involves your thoughts and emotions,*
> *the chemical reactions in your brain and your body,*
> *and the resulting physical sensations.*

The power of negative thinking

The stress reaction or stress cycle begins with your thoughts. You may have believed that it is the number of problems you have in your life or how serious these are that determines how stressed you get, but it is not. It is how you think about them. It is not the events in your life that cause you emotional stress but the way in which you interpret them.

You may find this hard to believe, but look at it this way. Take an event that for most people would be very stressful: losing your job. If you think, 'It's a disaster, what will I do?', you will be stressed. But if you think, 'I'm going to set up my own business now; this has really given me the push I needed', you won't be stressed.

It is your thoughts that call the shots on your emotions and determine the physical changes in your body that accompany stress. Negative thoughts, in particular those that imply some loss of control on your part, have a power that far outreaches that of positive thinking. Once you start to think negatively, you are locked into a sequence that is as inevitable as the tide.

> *It is not what happens that causes you stress but how you think about it.*

The stress cycle
Stage 1: Negative thoughts

Stage 1 of the stress cycle is the thought. Thoughts start in the upper layer of your brain, the cortex or centre for rational thinking. But it is not just any thought that will upset you. If you think positive or coping thoughts, you won't be stressed. Stress follows only when you think negatively about whatever is bothering you. If your thought is one that will cause you some emotional discomfort, and especially if it implies an inability to cope or a loss of control on your part, the rest of the stress cycle will be set off.

If you're leaving home for the first time, or if you're breaking up a relationship, and you think, 'Thank God! Free at last', you won't experience stress as it is defined in this book. But if you think, 'How will I manage on my own? Who will support me?', the rest of the stress cycle will follow. Your emotions will lead to significant changes in your body, and you're likely to feel your life is getting out of control.

> *Stress follows only when you think negatively about whatever is bothering you.*

Fig. 2 The stress reaction

THE THOUGHT   THE EMOTION
'I CAN'T HANDLE THIS'   ANXIETY

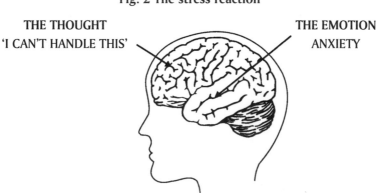

Stages 1 & 2: Negative thoughts and emotions

Stage 2: Negative emotions

The thought that starts in your cortex continues to activate other nerve cells in a pathway down into an area of your mid-brain, the limbic system. This is thought to be where your emotions lie.

Stage 2 of the stress cycle is the emotion. Negative thoughts produce negative emotions; positive thoughts don't. It's as simple as that. The content or the nature of your thought determines exactly what emotion you will feel. For example, if you think, 'The boss bawled me out and he had no right to do that', you will feel angry. If you think, 'The boss bawled me out and I'd better pull my socks up', you will probably feel anxious. Of course, if you think, 'The boss bawled me out, but I know he doesn't really mean it', then you won't be upset at all, you won't feel any negative emotion, and Stages 3 and 4 of the stress cycle will not be set off.

Humans can experience many, many different negative emotions in response to stressful thoughts. There's fear, anger, guilt, hatred, envy, regret, remorse, grief, sadness, suspicion, disappointment, anxiety, depression, jealousy and embarrassment, and I'm sure you can think of even more. But although you can distinguish between the emotions you feel, the next stage of the stress cycle is almost exactly the same no matter what negative emotion you're feeling, just so long as it is negative.

(Note: Researchers are still debating whether emotions are the second or the fourth stage in the stress cycle. A different view from the one presented here holds that you must feel the physical changes in your body [Stage 3] before you can experience the emotion.)

> *Negative thoughts produce negative emotions.*

Stage 3: Chemical reactions

Stage 3 of the stress cycle involves both your nervous system and your endocrine or hormonal system. It is a very general reaction; much the same events occur no matter what negative emotion you're feeling. You'll get the same reaction whether you're feeling angry, sad, frightened, embarrassed, guilty or grief stricken.

At Stage 3 the negative thoughts that have reached your limbic system send nerve impulses to the adrenal gland on your kidneys. This speeds up the action of many of your organs and triggers the release of a number of different chemicals into your bloodstream. These chemicals circulate right through your body, and on their way affect another gland, your pituitary gland, which is located under part of your brain, the hypothalamus; it triggers the release of still more hormones and chemicals from your adrenal gland. These are all very generally known as the stress chemicals. Probably one of the best known is epinephrine or adrenaline, but there are others as well: norepinephrine, serotonin, and a variety of cortico-steroids. Some are neurotransmitters, the chemicals involved in neural transmission in the brain, and others are hormones. (Recent research indicates that you may experience slightly different physical symptoms in your body depending on the emotion you are feeling.)

Fig. 3 The stress reaction

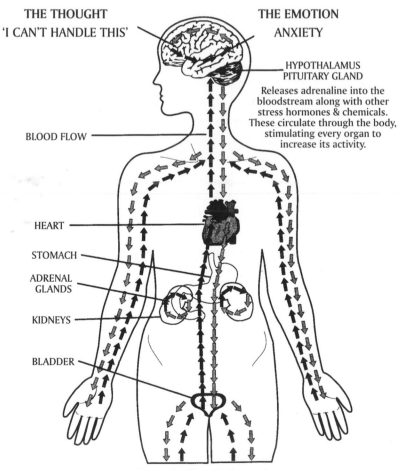

THE THOUGHT
'I CAN'T HANDLE THIS'

THE EMOTION
ANXIETY

HYPOTHALAMUS
PITUITARY GLAND

Releases adrenaline into the bloodstream along with other stress hormones & chemicals. These circulate through the body, stimulating every organ to increase its activity.

BLOOD FLOW

HEART

STOMACH

ADRENAL GLANDS

KIDNEYS

BLADDER

Stage 3: Chemical reactions

The net result of this nervous system activity and all these chemicals is to activate every single organ in your body to work faster. Your heart pounds, your digestion speeds up, your breathing becomes more rapid. You notice it most when you are feeling very intense emotion like fear or anger, but even when you are thinking a slightly upsetting thought, the same process is happening. It is as though your body is receiving a huge burst of energy and being mobilised for action; you can often feel a hot rising surge run through you. Once the stress chemicals are released, everything goes on red alert and it is at this point that you actually feel the physical symptoms of stress in the form of changes in your body.

Fig. 4 The stress reaction

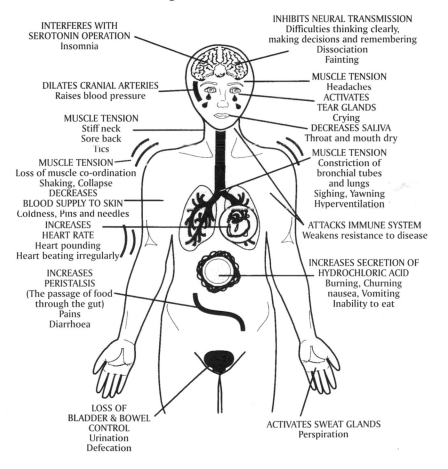

INTERFERES WITH
SEROTONIN OPERATION
Insomnia

INHIBITS NEURAL TRANSMISSION
Difficulties thinking clearly,
making decisions and remembering
Dissociation
Fainting

DILATES CRANIAL ARTERIES
Raises blood pressure

MUSCLE TENSION
Headaches
ACTIVATES
TEAR GLANDS
Crying

MUSCLE TENSION
Stiff neck
Sore back
Tics

DECREASES SALIVA
Throat and mouth dry

MUSCLE TENSION
Loss of muscle co-ordination
Shaking, Collapse
DECREASES
BLOOD SUPPLY TO SKIN
Coldness, Pins and needles

MUSCLE TENSION
Constriction of
bronchial tubes
and lungs
Sighing, Yawning
Hyperventilation

INCREASES
HEART RATE
Heart pounding
Heart beating irregularly

ATTACKS IMMUNE SYSTEM
Weakens resistance to disease

INCREASES
PERISTALSIS
(The passage of food
through the gut)
Pains
Diarrhoea

INCREASES SECRETION OF
HYDROCHLORIC ACID
Burning, Churning
nausea, Vomiting
Inability to eat

LOSS OF
BLADDER & BOWEL
CONTROL
Urination
Defecation

ACTIVATES SWEAT GLANDS
Perspiration

Stage 4: Physical symptoms

> *Once stress chemicals are released, everything goes on red alert.*
> *Every organ in your body is activated to work faster.*

Stage 4: Physical symptoms

The physical symptoms that you, as an individual, are aware of when you are stressed depend primarily on two things:

*   how intense an emotion you are feeling – the more you see your situation as upsetting or beyond your control, the greater the amount of chemicals released, and the more physical changes you will notice; and
*   where your particular body manifests its stress most. While you may notice your heart pounding when you are upset, your neighbour may be more aware of butterflies or churning in the stomach. Nonetheless, your stomach will also be churning, whether you're conscious of it or not.

> *The physical symptoms you notice when you are stressed depend*
> *on how intense an emotion you are feeling and where your body*
> *shows its stress most.*

The following are the changes that occur:

Heart

When you're under stress, your heart rate increases and your blood circulates more rapidly through your body. You will often feel that your heart is thumping or pounding or beating irregularly or missing a beat. Sometimes you may get palpitations: your heart races so wildly that you are sure it will burst.

Stomach

The stress chemicals activate your stomach to produce hydrochloric acid in order to digest your food. Normally this happens only when you have food in your stomach, but when you're stressed, acid flows continuously. This is why you may feel butterflies or burning or churning or nausea in your stomach when you're emotionally upset: Sometimes you may feel unable to eat when you're badly stressed; occasionally you may even vomit.

Gut

The stress chemicals also speed up peristalsis, the passage of food through your gut. You may experience pain in your lower stomach or diarrhoea when you are emotionally upset. You're also more likely to want to urinate, because your kidney function will be speeded up. This is why soldiers in war, under intense fear, often suffer a complete loss of bladder and bowel function.

Muscles

Every single muscle in your body constricts when you're stressed. Some of the physical effects of this are headaches, stiff necks, and sore backs and muscle tics. You may also notice a sensation like a tight band around your chest, and a general feeling of muscle tension. Under very great stress your muscle co-ordination can be totally lost and you may find that you're shaking and trembling. You can even give way at the knees and collapse when you're extremely upset.

Breathing

Your lungs and your bronchial tubes are also constricted when you're under stress, so all the apparatus through which you breathe becomes compressed. You may experience irregularities in your breathing; your body finds it hard to get enough oxygen when everything is tensed up. Sometimes you may notice you're sighing a lot; at other times you may yawn. Under extreme stress you may hyperventilate. This is the fast, shallow, panting sort of breathing that makes you light-headed and dizzy.

Tear glands

Your stress chemicals activate your tear glands, making it more likely that you will cry when you're upset. You may not always cry about the problem that's on your mind, but you often find you're bursting into tears at sad movies or upsetting events on the news. This can even happen when you're brooding on something that's making you angry, because the same chemicals are released and the same physical changes happen whether you're angry or sad.

Sweat glands

Your sweat glands are also stimulated when you're under stress. This is your body's attempt to maintain a normal body temperature in the face of heightened blood circulation. It's the reason you'll often find that your hands are clammy when you're upset, or you break out in a sweat on your forehead or under your arms.

Saliva

The flow of saliva decreases when you're stressed, your throat and your mouth become dry, and swallowing is difficult.

Skin

Initially stress speeds up the blood flow to your skin, which is why you'll often notice a flushing or red rash when you're under stress. This is probably most obvious when you're embarrassed. Later, though, the blood flow to the capillaries in your skin is decreased and more of your blood than normal is restricted to the central core of your body. This is when you're likely to feel cold or to notice you've gone white. Some people even get pins and needles or tingling in their extremities because of the reduced blood flow there when they are stressed.

Menstrual cycle

Under prolonged stress and certainly during depression, you can experience disturbances in your menstrual functioning. Periods are often more painful and frequently they become irregular or absent. Sometimes they may be lighter or heavier than normal.

Sexual problems

Stress directs the flow of your blood into the central part of your body rather than your extremities and it tenses your muscles. Sexual arousal requires blood in the extremities of your body – an erection is blood in the penis; the clitoris is insensitive without a blood supply – and a relaxed muscle tone. Lack of sexual desire, painful intercourse and vaginal muscle spasms, and a lack of orgasm and ejaculation are common when you're stressed.

Brain

The brain exercises the greatest power in mankind,
but the air supplies sense to it.

HIPPOCRATES

The stress chemicals have a number of very profound effects on your brain. First they dilate your cranial arteries, the arteries that go into your brain. You may not feel the effects of this directly unless you're susceptible to migraine headaches but, as you will see later, dilation of the cranial arteries over a long period has some very serious physical consequences.

The direct effect of the stress chemicals on your brain is to make it difficult for you to think clearly and to remember. This is because some of the stress chemicals actually interfere with neural transmission, the passage of information through the brain, making it harder for your brain to operate and process the messages it receives.

Thinking and memory are, in part, chemical processes. The nerve cells in your brain have numerous fibres attached to them and the nerve impulse passes from cell to cell via these fibres. One fibre meets another at what is known as the synapse (from the Greek synapsis or junction). Cell fibres don't touch each other at their synapses; to jump over the gap between fibres, the first cell releases a chemical called a neurotransmitter into the gap. This neurotransmitter is then picked up by receptor proteins on the surface of the second cell. It fits the receptor as a key fits a lock, and as soon as it unlocks the receptor, this leads to the continuation of the nerve impulse to the second cell.

The stress chemicals interfere with the action of these neurotransmitters so that the nerve impulses in your brain are not properly transmitted, making your thinking and memory less efficient. In addition to this, your constricted lungs can't take in enough of the oxygen that is essential to thinking and memory. A restriction of the amount of oxygen your brain gets also interferes with its ability to operate properly.

The interference with your neurotransmitters and the reduction of oxygen to your brain cause quite specific effects. When you are very stressed, you may find that you can't make decisions, you can't think clearly or you can't concentrate on what you're supposed to be doing. Your head feels fuzzy. This is why when something is very important to you, at the time when you most need to make a rational decision, you are least able to – or if you force yourself to decide, you'll often agonise over it afterwards, wondering whether you've made the best decision.

When you're stressed you'll also often notice that you're forgetting things. You walk into a room and think 'What did I come in here for?' You go to introduce your best friend to someone and find you've forgotten their name. Stage fright is, for many people, a familiar example of forgetfulness caused by stress. If you get up to speak in front of a group of people and go totally blank, it's because the stress chemicals have knocked out your neurotransmitters and affected your memory.

> *Stress chemicals make it difficult for you to think clearly,*
> *concentrate, make decisions and to remember.*
> *Stress also interferes with sleep.*

Difficulties sleeping are also common when you're emotionally upset. This is because the stress chemicals also interfere with the production of serotonin, one of the neurotransmitters that is involved in sleep. Sometimes you can't go to sleep, but more often you will drop off all right, sleep for a few hours, and then wake for an hour or two before you can go back to sleep again. Or you may wake at 4 a.m. and stay awake for the rest of the night. Almost always you'll find you're on red alert and thinking the most negative of thoughts when you wake in the middle of the night. Read on if you want to find out why this is so.

Under very intense stress you may experience what is known as dissociation, a feeling of unreality, as though you're not even in your body any more, but hovering above it, watching yourself. People who report themselves to have been paralysed with fear are probably in this condition. It is due to the interference with brain function caused by the stress chemicals. You can even become dizzy and faint or lose consciousness totally under the most extreme stress.

Panic attacks

Under intense or prolonged stress you may experience a panic attack. These are extremely frightening, and often take the form of intense, recurring spasms of panic that start just below the breastbone, and seem to spread all over the body. Your heart also beats frantically, your breathing is rapid and your body feels as though it is running on automatic without you having any control over it.

Panic attacks are sometimes triggered by an apparently minor event, but if you look carefully you'll find you've been under stress without controlling it for a long time. The trigger for the attack was just the proverbial straw that broke the camel's back. Once a panic attack starts, the symptoms can often be so frightening that thoughts like, 'What on earth is happening to me? … Am I having a heart attack? … I must be dying!' flood into your head. Through thinking these thoughts, you will continue your attack: more chemicals pour into your bloodstream, and more panic symptoms follow.

Immune system

Stress chemicals also attack your immune system, which protects you from disease. It is composed of many different kinds of specialised cells known as leucocytes, or white blood cells, that originate in your bone marrow and then migrate to various organs in your body: your thymus, spleen and lymph nodes. Leucocytes are released into the blood from these organs and they may also return there when they have done their job of identifying and eliminating foreign materials that come into contact with or enter your body. These foreign bodies include viruses, parasites, bacteria and fungi. Some cells in the immune system are also able to identify and destroy mutant cells, which are cells that have undergone alterations that make them malignant – cancer cells.

> *Some chemicals released during the stress reaction destroy the cells of your immune system, leaving you with reduced protection against disease.*

The merry-go-round of stress

> *Pleasure is oft a visitant;*
> *but pain clings cruelly to us.*
>
> JOHN KEATS

The stress reaction is not a start-stop process. In fact it's a bit like a merry-go-round; it's a process that's very hard to halt once it begins. But why is this? One of the most interesting and significant things about the stress reaction is that it is self-perpetuating. Once you start to get stressed, your body is not designed to make that stress stop easily. Stress truly feeds upon itself. How does this happen?

> *Once you start to get stressed, the process is hard to stop.*

How stress feeds on itself

The part of your nervous system which fires off the first barrage of your stress cycle is known as the sympathetic nervous system. It speeds the action of some of your organs, like your heart, itself, but it also releases the chemicals from your adrenal gland which increase the speeding up of all your organs. There is another branch of this system known as the parasympathetic nervous system whose role is to calm down your speeding organs. Unfortunately, this doesn't work very effectively because many of the stress chemicals that are released by negative thinking are biochemically and psychologically depressant in their action. This means that as soon as they start to circulate through your brain, every new thought that enters into your head is going to be emotionally negative. This starts you off on a whole cycle of negative thinking; it stimulates your sympathetic nervous system again and keeps the cycle going. Does this scenario sound familiar?

Why can't you stop the merry-go-round?

Grief and disappointment give rise to anger, anger to envy, envy to malice and malice to grief again till the whole circle be completed.

DAVID HUME

Let's say you've just received a letter from the bank manager about your account. You might start off thinking, 'I've overdrawn my cheque account again; that's not smart.' This is the original thought that triggers off your stress. Your next thoughts might go something like this: 'I'm really worried about money; I don't seem to be managing well at all … I can't ever seem to do anything right … Work's not going the way I want it to either. I said that stupid thing yesterday to the boss; she must think I'm a real incompetent … Everything I touch turns to dust. My whole life is a mess at the moment. It's pointless living.'

Each of these separate thoughts gives you another shot of stress chemicals, intensifies your physical symptoms and is responsible for even more negative, black thoughts. The longer you dwell on your problems the more upsetting, irrational and paranoid your thoughts become. You may start off feeling mildly upset over something and end up 30 minutes later wanting to slit your throat. This is why you'll find yourself thinking your blackest thoughts when you're lying awake in the middle of the night. There's nothing to distract you and take your mind off your problems, and so you'll continue to dwell on them and to magnify them.

*The longer you dwell on your problems the more upsetting,
irrational and paranoid your thoughts become.
Once you're upset, every other unpleasant emotion you feel
will be more extreme.*

The cyclic nature of the stress reaction also explains why you get angry over trivia if you're already stressed about something else. Once you're upset, every other unpleasant emotion you feel will be more extreme. If you've missed a deadline at work and you're worried about facing the boss tomorrow, when you get home and find the washing machine is broken down or the television is on the blink you'll be furious. If you're worried about money and someone asks you to take on a new project at work, you're likely to be far more anxious about doing it than if money wasn't constantly on your mind.

The more circulating stress chemicals you have, the more intensely you'll feel any negative emotion and the greater the range of negative emotions you're likely to have.

Why does your body do this to you? It hardly seems a good response, and for many people it's a very frightening one. The symptoms are powerful and sometimes they can feel so intense you may genuinely wonder whether you're physically ill. At other times you're so unable to cope you may think you're having a mental breakdown.

Distressing thoughts, unpleasant emotions and major physical changes in your body are perfectly normal when you're stressed. They happen to everybody. In our distant past they ensured the survival of the species. But now they are often extremely inconvenient. And, as you will see, the whole process has some pretty serious side effects.

The fight/flight reaction

The stress cycle is sometimes known by another name: the fight/flight reaction. Although the human brain has developed over the last 100,000 years, the stress reaction has not. Early humans' bodies reacted in exactly the same way to emotions as yours does today, but for them the fight/flight reaction was extremely useful. Its original purpose was to supply a huge shot of energy to mobilise your body to take some physical action. However, for early humans probably the only significant negative emotion was fear. The trigger for your fear was likely to be the bear at the cave door and you would have needed the energy supplied by the stress chemicals to fight it or to flee from it; hence the term fight/flight reaction.

You can see too that the self-perpetuating nature of the fight/flight reaction was very useful because it kept on supplying the energy needed for the fight – or the flight. The more early humans thought, 'Help, I'm losing!' or, 'Its hot breath is on my neck!', the more stress chemicals would shoot into the bloodstream, and the more energy would be available. When the need was over, the person's thinking probably changed to, 'Great! Got away!' or 'Great! Food for the next week', which would have triggered the parasympathetic nervous system and switched off the whole reaction.

> *The fight/flight reaction was intended to help early humans spring into action when faced with danger. Today, however, our problems are more complex and the reaction is triggered more frequently.*

Today, however, this fight/flight reaction is triggered far more frequently than it was in earlier times. Humans have many more negative emotions now than fear. It is totally inappropriate to react to these more subtle emotions – embarrassment, envy, grief, regret, guilt, and so on – with any extreme physical action. Our emotions have developed since we lived in caves, but the mechanisms with which they are expressed have not.

In the twenty-first century, you don't in most cases need the energy supplied by the fight/flight reaction when you get upset, but when you don't get rid of this energy in some way, your body is continually mobilised for an action that never comes. It's also harder today to tell when you've killed the bear. Today's problems are more complex than that and so we continue to dwell on the thoughts that set the cycle off. The longer you think about what is stressing you, the more negative your thinking becomes and the more the adrenaline and other chemicals pour into your bloodstream and keep you on red alert.

What happens when you can't get off the merry-go-round?

Nothing vivifies and nothing kills like the emotions.

JOSEPH ROUX

To say the least, the acute physical arousal produced by the stress reaction is not good for your body. It becomes exhausted. Have you noticed how tired you get when you're under stress? Even if you're managing to sleep, you'll feel drained and unmotivated; life's a struggle. It's no wonder, when you think about it, as all your organs are working twice as fast as they should. Your body is running a marathon, but you're going nowhere.

> *Uncontrolled, the stress reaction can be extremely harmful, and not just to your body. Stress affects the way you behave more directly than making you exhausted. It can change your personality, interfere with your relationships and take away your confidence.*

Both physical and mental illnesses result from long-term stress. Your quality of life may drop, decisions become difficult, setting goals – and reaching them – becomes a thing of the past. Worst of all, you create more stress for yourself; it's not only the stress cycle that is self-perpetuating, so are its effects. Stress that is unattended is rather like your grandmother's home-made ginger beer. It is just sitting there in the bottle, but all the time it's fermenting away, and if you don't take the top off in time, one day it explodes and blows the whole bottle apart. If you are stressed, you're out of control of your life in many ways, some of them major and potentially irreversible. The longer you're in this state, the more out of control you get.

Let's look at the harmful effects of long-term stress in some detail. First, stress can give you a vast array of physical ailments and illnesses. It can also affect you mentally. At best these disorders seriously limit your ability to live a happy and fulfilling life; at worst some of them can kill you.

Your body falls apart

You can choose the manner of your death by the way in which you live. Stress wears your body out before its time, producing real physical disorders. Physical and mental health are inextricably entwined, as increasing amounts of medical and psychological research make clear. If you're stressed or depressed for too long, or if you're the kind of person who's always been described as 'nervy' or 'a worrier' or 'someone with an attitude or an anger problem', and you're constantly getting upset about things, you are putting a major strain on your body. Something is likely to break down.

> *Stress wears your body out before its time,*
> *producing physical disorders.*

Ultimately your body can't take constant mobilisation. Eventually exhaustion sets in. Hormones that have been produced at abnormally high rates become depleted, as do important trace minerals, particularly potassium. When this happens your cells no longer receive enough nutrients and they start to die. Organs in your body that may have been weakened by previous illnesses or stress can fail and threaten your survival. Everyone has a weak link in the chain of organs that keep the body operating, and if you are under stress too often, or for too long at any one time, that's the place that will break down.

Your weak link

If your weak link is your heart, you may end up with heart attacks. Your heart won't take the strain of operating at above normal rates for too long. If it's your lungs, you can develop asthma or worsen the asthma you already have, because stress restricts your airways. If your weak link is your stomach, you can develop ulcers; the hydrochloric acid secreted during stress not only digests your food but ultimately interacts with certain bacteria in your stomach to digest the lining of your stomach. If your gut is your vulnerable spot, stress gives you irritable bowel and colitis. If it's your skin, you can break out in spots, eczema, dermatitis, alopecia, dandruff, or your hair falls out. Stress can also trigger outbreaks of skin disorders like herpes and shingles. If you're unlucky enough for your cranial arteries to be vulnerable, their constant dilation by the stress reaction may result in migraines or high blood pressure. Ultimately this can cause your arteries to perforate and you suffer a stroke.

Fig. 5 The stress reaction

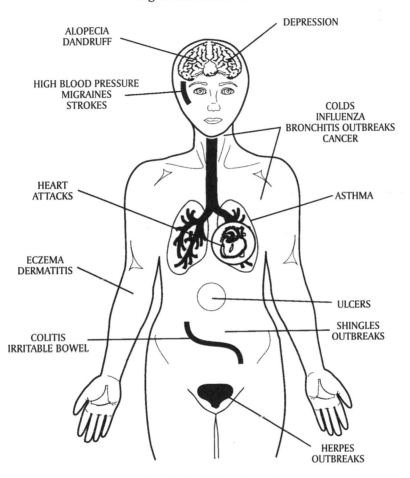

The physical disorders of stress

Interestingly, it's not only humans who have these stress-related ailments, animals do too.

> *If you are under stress too often, or for too long, the weak link in your chain of organs will break.*

If your weak link in the chain of organs that keep your body functioning is the neurotransmitter and neuroendocrine systems of your brain you may develop depression, burnout, phobias or anxiety disorders. Mental illnesses like schizophrenia, obsessive compulsive disorder and manic depression, while not caused by stress, can be triggered by it. If you are predisposed to these disorders, stress will often set off an episode. Although we may fear and denigrate people with mental illnesses, we do so only because we endow the effects of prolonged or intense stress that occur in the brain with different meanings than those that occur, say, in the stomach or any other part of the body. All are just body malfunctions. It's really only the luck of the draw that determines whether your stress will produce an ulcer or cancer, or trigger a crippling episode of schizophrenia.

> *If you be sick, your own thoughts make you sick.*
>
> BEN JONSON

Weakened immune system

> *My problem is I internalise everything.*
> *I don't express anger; I grow a tumour instead.*
>
> WOODY ALLEN

If your immune system is weakened by the stress chemicals, you can become vulnerable to all manner of illnesses, minor and major. It used to be thought that most diseases floated about in the air in the form of germs or bacteria, and if you were unlucky enough to come into contact with these, you got sick. Now we know that is not true. Although there are diseases that are contagious, medical science has established that many of the viruses and bacteria that cause illness reside within your body all the time and only manifest themselves when your immune system is low. This is why, when your life is out of control, or when the pressure is on you most, you're also likely to get sick. You'll come down with colds, influenza, bronchitis, pneumonia or some other complaint.

What about cancer? It is often claimed that stress is a cause of cancer, and there is some truth in this.

According to the immune surveillance theory, cancer is the result of an immune system malfunction. This theory says that the mutations that start cancer are a common occurrence in everyone, with mutant cells normally killed off by one particular type of leucocyte or immune system cell. Cancer occurs when stress has destroyed those cells in the immune system that identify and destroy mutant cells. Stress doesn't actually give you cancer, but it does markedly reduce your ability to fight it off, and to fight off every other illness that's going around. No matter what illness you have, you will combat it more effectively if you manage your stress.

Researchers have identified a formidable list of disorders that appear to be caused or made worse by stress. Besides the mental disorders, sudden cardiac deaths, myocardial infarction, hypertension, cancer, strokes, influenza, pneumonia and herpes mentioned earlier, gastro-intestinal disorders, diabetes, multiple sclerosis, auto-immune disorders, rheumatoid arthritis, and AIDS are all more likely if you are chronically stressed, depressed or lonely.

> *Many disorders are more likely if you are chronically stressed, depressed or lonely.*

Your personality and your behaviour changes

Personality problems

> *The intellect is always fooled by the heart.*
> DUC DE LA ROCHEFOUCAULD

When you're under stress, particularly for a long time, you may notice many unpleasant changes in your character. Sometimes you don't see them yourself; others have to tell you. These changes in your personality also affect the way you behave. If you were an optimist, you might mutate into a pessimist or a defeatist or a worrier who sees the world as a hostile, difficult place. You may become more irritable and touchy with your friends and your family and your work colleagues. You might become prone to anger outbursts that are guaranteed to undermine your relationships.

Flooded with self-doubt, you begin to worry about your ability to run your life. Suddenly your self-esteem is plummeting down to zero, leaving you bereft of confidence. Envy and jealousy beset you. Things you used to do with ease, you're scared to even attempt. You may find your eating patterns change, or you're drinking too much, or using drugs. How do these major changes in behaviour come about?

Because some of the stress chemicals are biochemical and psychological depressants, the longer you dwell on your woes, the more defeatist, black and paranoid your thinking becomes. Every negative emotion is intensified. Objectivity flies out the window. As far as you're concerned, the whole world is against you.

If you feel more pessimistic, you'll act with anxious caution and with no expectations of a positive outcome. To the pessimist, the only light at the end of the tunnel is an approaching train. If you feel angrier, of course you'll act more aggressively. You may regret it later, but you won't be rational at the time you're provoked.

There is an intimate relationship between stress and low self-esteem. When you are not managing your stress, you lose your confidence. You think of yourself as an individual composed entirely of flaws and weaknesses. You not only think negatively about your life and your problems but about yourself and your ability to cope with what's happening to you. If you feel insecure, you'll compare yourself unfavourably with others, and you'll act out of envy and jealousy. Since you've convinced yourself that you are incapable of meeting the challenges of life, you won't even try. If you're prey to fear, then everything that disquiets you will escalate into dread. Existing phobias become worse under stress, and new ones develop.

> *I've been scared of heights since I was a little kid but never had any other phobias until quite recently. We bought a café – thought it was a good business but we lost money right from the start. It was terrible, I was so worried – all our savings were going down the drain, we couldn't sell it and we couldn't close it because we had to pay the lease. The stress was enormous. I felt panicky all the time – I developed a phobia about driving over the Harbour Bridge, then I became terrified about driving in rush hour traffic. I ended up being scared even to go out of my front door.*

Being under stress, particularly for a long time, can change your personality, which will affect the way you behave.

No man can think clearly when his fists are clenched.
GEORGE JEAN NATHAN

Relationship problems

Even love is tainted by stress. As the proverb says: 'When poverty comes in the door, love flies out the window.' You're more likely to fall out of love when you're stressed, because you'll think negatively about your lover, as well as about everything else in your life.

What is love? The dictionary defines it as: 'to like or desire something very much; wholehearted liking for or pleasure in something'. Love is about seeing the positive qualities and not the negative, or at least, not only the negative. Love is definitely in the eye of the beholder. If you see mostly the things you like in your lover you will love him or her. You will have the goodwill to overlook the flaws and the failings, and the goodwill to negotiate and compromise and forgive when you have an argument. If you see mostly the weaknesses and the qualities you dislike, you'll fall out of love. You won't want to compromise in an argument. You'll want to prove that you're right, you'll want to win. And if either partner in a relationship wins an argument, the relationship usually loses.

Under stress you take a negative view of everything, including your partner. Little things they do annoy you intensely. What used to be charming becomes irritating. Arguments increase, alienation from each other intensifies. You make your lover behave badly because you take out your stress on them, criticising or picking fights. You stop wanting to make the effort to put the relationship back on track. As you start seeing the other person differently, the rosy glow fades; you see none of the good qualities, only the bad. One morning you wake up and think – who is this stranger? How could I ever have loved this person?

By the time I realised I'd fallen out of love, everything she did irritated me. It wasn't fair, but little things would drive me crazy. Like the way she cleaned her teeth – she'd let the toothpaste run out of her mouth and drip down her chin into the basin. It had never bothered me before, but it got to the point I couldn't even stand to be in the bathroom with her.

> Under stress you take a negative view of everything, including your partner. You take out your stress on them, criticising or picking fights.

Depression

If stress is prolonged or very intense, it is highly likely that unless you know how to manage your stress, you will become depressed. In the Introduction the relationship between loss of control and depression was outlined. When your stress has become beyond your ability to control, then you become helpless and depression may follow. There is a difference between stress and depression, although stress generally precedes depression and quite a lot of the physical symptoms of stress remain when you are depressed. The most obvious differences are in the kind of emotion you feel when you are depressed, and in the intensity of your depression, which is likely to vary throughout the day.

> *When your stress has become beyond your ability to control, then depression – a sense of overriding hopelessness and despair – may follow.*

The emotion that accompanies depression is often hard to label accurately because you can't pinpoint exactly what you're feeling. It is not anxiety or fear or frustration, although sometimes these may still be present but there is a sense of overriding hopelessness and despair, a belief that nothing will ever go well again. Life tastes like cardboard, and often you can't feel anything very intensely. Your sensibilities seem blunted regardless of what else is going on. You can't concentrate on anything. You can't be bothered with other people. You lack the motivation not only to do the things you should do but even the things you used to like doing. You feel constantly exhausted; you do not enjoy anything anymore. Shakespeare, in *Hamlet*, described the feelings very accurately: 'How weary, stale, flat and unprofitable, seem to me all the uses of this world.'

Depression is generally worse first thing in the morning and lifts throughout the day, although sometimes it is the evenings that are the worst. You may wake up feeling so ghastly and unable to cope that you can't get out of bed and face the day. By nightfall life may seem tolerable, but next morning dawns as dreadful as the one before it. These changes in mood occur apparently independently of whatever else is going on in your day.

There is some evidence now that prolonged stress upsets your circadian rhythms. When this happens depression results. Circadian rhythms, more familiarly known as biorhythms, are the biological changes that occur or vary in your body, most within about a 24-hour interval, but some, like the menstrual cycle, within a longer period. These biological processes, which include sleeping, appetite, body temperature, metabolic rate, urination and defecation, sexual functioning, and your moods are caused by fluctuations in the hormone levels in your blood. Some of these hormones are the same ones released during stress. The level of these hormones in your bloodstream is normally regulated by a nucleus, or cluster of cells, in your brain. Some researchers now think that when you become depressed it is because this regulatory process has been thrown out by the stress reaction. You can see that this explains why you get menstrual cycle irregularities under prolonged stress.

> *There is evidence that prolonged stress upsets your biorhythms, and this causes depression.*

Similar feelings to depression can occur for shorter periods with jet-lag and with shift-work, because long distance air travel and irregular sleep patterns can also throw out your biorhythms.

Researchers are unsure exactly how stress alters the biorhythms and causes depression. It may be that the hormones that are secreted during a prolonged period of stress become depleted, that your body just cannot go on producing them; there is some evidence that this is the case. The regulatory nucleus itself may also be involved. What is sure is that if you're prescribed antidepressants for your depression, they act on the chemicals and hormones involved in regulating your biorhythms, and should ultimately – within 14–28 days for most antidepressants – help to stabilise the variation in your moods and to lift the feelings of hopelessness. If you are clinically depressed rather than stressed, you may find that you need antidepressants before you can start to take control of your life. Of course, if you manage your stress in the ways described in this book you are not likely to become depressed.

Remember, though, if you do embark upon a course of antidepressants, you will still need to deal with the original causes of your stress or you will go back to being depressed once you stop the antidepressants.

You can't make decisions

There is no more miserable human being than one in whom nothing is habitual but indecision.

HENRY JAMES

The process of growing up and learning to run your life is a procedure in which you gradually assume more and more responsibility for your own decisions. When you are a child, there are many decisions you cannot make because your parents do not feel you have the wisdom, and so your parents control your life. When you are an adult, if you want to take over that control from them, you need to be able to make those decisions. If you are stressed you may not be able to.

Because some of the stress hormones and chemicals interfere with the action of your neurotransmitters, they affect your brain chemistry so that it is difficult for you to think clearly and to make rational decisions. It is a physical impossibility for you to be at your best intellectually when you are stressed. Your brain is not able to operate properly. You will not think as clearly or as rationally, nor will you remember as well as if you were calm and relaxed.

Stress can interfere with your ability to make decisions about your life, and to set your goals and achieve them.

Given a decision to make when you are stressed, you may go to and fro and be unable to decide on anything. Decisions that you should be making will be put on hold, or if you do take the plunge and make a decision, your thinking may be too confused for you to evaluate all your options impartially and your choice may be the wrong one. You may feel so paralysed mentally that you develop tunnel vision over your problems and you cannot see any solutions to them. You become unsure about what your goals should be and you doubt your ability to achieve them.

Many people have dismissed the effects of stress, saying such things as: 'Stress is all in your mind'. True, that's where it starts, but it does not stop there. It also causes real physical disorders and illnesses in your body. We know now that you can suffer anything from death to dandruff by being stressed, and we know why. Our Victorian forebears had no problem with the fact that people could die of a broken heart or of melancholy. Fortunately, we now know how to prevent it.

Stress stops you taking full control of your life and achieving to your full potential. Learning to manage your stress well will not only make you a healthier, happier, more confident and optimistic person, but it will allow you to live longer and to have a higher quality of life while you do so.

Summing Up

- To create your ideal life you must first know your human limitations. Out of control stress is the greatest of these.
- Negative thinking begins the loss of control.
- It sets off a cycle of negative emotions and harmful chemical and physical changes, right throughout your body.
- Once this starts you cannot stop it, you are on the merry-go-round.
- The end point of this cycle is not only unhappiness, it can be both mental and physical illness.

Are you one of the vulnerable?

The unexamined life is not worth living.

SOCRATES

Knowledge is power. This has never been more true than when it applies to self-knowledge. The more you know about yourself, the more you will have the power to control your own life. By the end of this book you will know more about yourself than you ever thought possible: you will be able to identify the thoughts that distress you and that limit your life, and comprehend their effects on your emotions and on your body. You will understand how these physical and emotional symptoms in turn are affecting your personality and your behaviour. You will be able to see what illnesses you're headed for if your stress continues unabated, and you'll also have some idea of the manner of your death if you don't do something about it.

> *The more you know about yourself, the more you will have the power to control your life.*

And you can do something. You can learn the skills to solve your problems. You can learn how to be philosophical about those you cannot solve. You will understand how to keep yourself calm, positive and optimistic. You will have a clear idea of your strengths and how important it is to focus on them, and you will know how to plan the kind of life you want to live.

Knowing your weaknesses

Know myself? If I knew myself, I'd run away.

GOETHE

Self-knowledge is not just about learning the skills and finding the strengths, though. You need to look at the full picture: assets and liabilities. Being aware of your vulnerabilities, the things that will hinder you from taking control of your life, is as much a part of the solution as knowing your strengths.

Many people are reluctant to confront their weaknesses; they fear knowing the darker side of themselves. But trying to manage your stress without understanding your liabilities is like hoping the garage can fix your car when you haven't told them everything that is wrong with it. You can't possibly get the best results.

> *Being aware of the things that will stop you from taking control of your life is as much a part of the solution as knowing your strengths.*

Are you ever baffled about why you get upset more easily than other people? Do you feel powerless in the tide of events that sweeps you away from the goals in your life? Do you feel a victim of circumstances: you know what you want, but it never happens? Do you think, 'Other people are lucky; they seem to get ahead, but I never do?' Do you give up easily and float with the current, convinced you never will get anywhere in life?

There is no doubt some people are more vulnerable to stress than others. The dice are loaded against them. These handicaps are both genetic and environmental: some you inherit, some are caused by your life experiences.

> *Vulnerability to stress can be inherited or caused by natural changes in the body or by life experiences.*

Weaknesses you are born with

The tendency to trigger off the stress reaction rapidly or not so rapidly is there when you are conceived and when you're born. Your nervous system's level of reactivity is inherited from your forebears. Some babies are born placid and some are born hyperactive and there is a wide range in between; you can see these differences clearly displayed from birth.

Even within the same family, children can differ enormously in their reactions to stress. Many a mother, after an 'easy' baby, has had a rude awakening the second time around. Expecting a baby that feeds well, sleeps through the night and rarely cries, you are confronted with a raging tyrant that won't settle, that cries from one feed to the next and gets by on no sleep at all.

Biochemical contributors to vulnerability

It is not only the inherited sensitivity of your nervous system that predisposes you to stress. Natural changes occurring in your body's biochemistry either as the result of illness or malfunction, or through the ageing process, can also do this.

Illnesses

Illnesses which may cause you to feel stressed or depressed include thyroid malfunctions, hypoglycaemia or low blood sugar, diseases of the adrenal glands and pituitary gland and diseases such as chronic fatigue syndrome, mononucleosis, and hepatitis.

Most of these conditions will be readily diagnosed and treated by your doctor and won't affect your stress levels permanently. But it is important that you recognise that part of the pessimistic way you're feeling about your life has its origin in your physical illness and that you need to address that illness as well as to manage your stress. However, the same recognition and treatment by your doctor may not be true for thyroid malfunctions.

Thyroid disorders

It is estimated that a high percentage of people with thyroid disorders are not aware of them and that underactive thyroid problems in particular are very common. One source estimates that as many as 40 percent of people may suffer from undiagnosed thyroid insufficiency.

If your body produces too much thyroid hormone, a condition called hyperthyroidism, your metabolic rate speeds up and you are may lose weight even though you are eating all the time. Your heart rate becomes rapid; you sweat more; you can't stand heat; and you may become irritable, anxious and tense.

If your body produces insufficient thyroid hormone, a condition called hypothyroidism, your metabolic rate slows down. You may put on weight; you lose your energy; you are always tired; you may notice your skin is dry, your hair is thinning and your nails are brittle; you become vulnerable to infection; you feel the cold; and you may become depressed, headachy and unable to concentrate or remember as well as you used to. These changes don't happen all at once, they take place gradually, sometimes over a period of years.

Ageing

While you may never experience thyroid malfunction, you will get older. If you are a woman in your forties, or sometimes earlier, you will start to lose your sex hormones: estrogen, progesterone and testosterone. This period of hormone decline is known as the peri-menopause. It occurs up to 10 years before the menopause proper. Recent research shows that by the time a woman is 40 she is producing only 50 percent of the testosterone she did in her twenties and less estrogen and progesterone also. If you are a man, from the age of 50 you too will be releasing lower and lower levels of testosterone in particular but also less of the other two hormones, estrogen and progesterone.

Your sex hormones perform multiple functions in your body – physical, mental and emotional. As you lose them, marked changes will occur, not just in your physical functioning, but in your thinking and in your emotions. Both men and women reach a point at which the body is no longer able to produce enough of these three hormones in the right balance to function optimally. In men, this has become known as the andropause. In women it is the menopause.

Because you lose these hormones at different rates (progesterone more rapidly than estrogen, and testosterone the most slowly), your body may not only display the symptoms of hormone deficiency, but of hormone imbalance or excess, particularly of estrogen excess as you get older. Your doctor will be familiar with the multitude of physical symptoms caused by these insufficiencies and imbalances and can explain their origins if you go for advice on such bodily changes as hot flushes, aches and pains, weight gain, urinary frequency, or lack of interest in sex. For that reason the full range of these physical symptoms is not described here. But your doctor may be less aware of the mental or emotional symptoms of hormone decline.

Before you read what follows it is important to note two things: first, even though your hormones may be out of balance, you won't necessarily experience all the symptoms listed here, and second, some of the symptoms of excesses of these hormones are identical to those found when your body is deficient in that same hormone.

Estrogen deficiency or excess

Estrogen deficiency may result in mental and emotional symptoms that include anxiety, depression, an inability to concentrate and memory problems.

If your body is making too much estrogen, or if you've lost too much of your progesterone and testosterone, you may find that you're irritable, you have mood swings, you're anxious, and you feel dizzy and sometimes confused mentally.

Progesterone deficiency or excess

Once your progesterone levels have dropped you are likely to feel anxious, irritable and depressed.

It is unlikely that you will experience symptoms of progesterone excess naturally since you lose your progesterone 12 times more rapidly than your estrogen. But if you are on hormone replacement therapy, and you are using too much progesterone, you may experience anything from mild sedation to depression.

Testosterone deficiency or excess

If your testosterone levels are too low you may feel depressed, you lose your enjoyment in life, you feel fatigued, you have no energy, and you will have a low sex drive.

If your body is making too much testosterone or if you are using too much in your hormone replacement you're likely to experience irritability, anger and difficulty sleeping.

Hormone-related disorders in women

Over and above the contribution to stress from the normal hormonal losses of ageing are certain hormonal conditions that may be experienced by women at any time in their life. Some of these involve excesses of hormones, some involve deficits.

Excess estrogen and its mood swings, anxiety, irritability, dizziness and mental confusion may be present if you have pre-menstrual syndrome, lupus, endometriosis, ovarian cysts, or fibroids.

You may have estrogen deficiency symptoms of anxiety, depression, poor concentration and memory problems, if you are postnatally depressed, have had a pregnancy termination, a tubal ligation, or a hysterectomy (with or without ovarian removal).

Progesterone deficiency symptoms of anxiety, irritability and depression may be present if you suffer from pre-menstrual syndrome, infertility, ovarian cysts, endometriosis, fibroids, postnatal depression, or if you have had a pregnancy termination, a hysterectomy (with or without ovarian removal), or a tubal ligation.

Excess testosterone symptoms of irritability, anger and insomnia may occur if you have polycystic ovarian disorder.

Testosterone deficiency symptoms such as depression, fatigue, loss of energy, a low sex drive and loss of enjoyment in your life may occur if you have had a hysterectomy (with or without the removal of your ovaries) or a tubal ligation.

Unless your hormones are in balance, you will find it a more uphill battle to be happy in your life even using the techniques outlined in this book.

> *If you are consistently stressed, irritable or depressed and think there may be a hormonal reason for the way you feel, consult your doctor.*

The effects of life

On top of your genetic predisposition to be calm or easily stressed are laid the effects of the experiences that happen to you right from the time of conception through your childhood and adulthood. There is no doubt that some experiences bias you towards over-reacting to stress; they turn you into someone who is anxious, or easily angered, or lacking in confidence. While it is difficult to separate out the effects of nature and nurture we do know that the events that occur throughout your childhood can have a profound effect on how well you cope with stress as an adult. If you are born placid, but you experience a traumatic childhood, the gentle stream of your emotions becomes a raging torrent. If you're born with a tendency to get upset very easily, and life deals you a bad hand on top of that, then you're likely to have a major struggle to keep yourself calm and in control as an adult. Psychologists call this double jeopardy.

Recent research suggests that stressful experiences even before your birth, as well as in childhood, are harmful to your later ability to cope with stress as an adult and to create a fulfilling life.

> *Stressful events before birth and in childhood can have a profound effect on how well you cope with stress as an adult.*

Stress affects brain development

> *Children need role models*
> *Rather than critics.*
>
> JOSEPH JOUBERT

According to the work of Bruce Perry, internationally known medical researcher at Baylor College of Medicine in Texas, and of many other scientists, the human brain develops according to the nature and patterning of the stimulation it receives. The implications of this are quite enormous. Your brain begins its development two weeks after conception. If you are a baby growing in the womb of a woman who is a victim of domestic violence, someone whose life is full of fear and terror, your brain will receive through the placenta enormous doses of your mother's stress chemicals. You will be born with a brain already exquisitely sensitive to stress.

Because your brain continues to grow and develop throughout your childhood and adolescence, the experiences you receive then continue to mould it. You may think that children will grow out of or get over the harmful things that happen to them in childhood but that is not generally true. As Perry says, it is the ultimate irony that at the time when the human brain is most vulnerable to the effects of trauma, adults presume the most resilience. A large number of independent studies in the last few years have shown that people who have been victims of major traumas in childhood, as adults have major and selective atrophy of part of their brain: the hippocampus. The hippocampus is involved in learning and memory. Some of the chemicals released during stress – glucocorticoids, are known to kill off the neurons in the hippocampus.

> *The brain grows faster in a stimulating and caring environment.*
> *A stressful environment can slow brain growth.*

Of course the reverse also occurs. If you are exposed to favourable stimulation as a baby and young child you will grow a more competent and resilient brain. According to Dr Robin Fancourt, who has worked with Bruce Perry, 'the brain literally grows faster in a stimulating and caring environment. An eight-month-old baby could have 25 percent more brain connections than an understimulated child. A two-year-old surrounded by caring adults may know 300 more words than a deprived child'.

Just how do your earlier experiences continue to affect your later level of stress? If you think back to the self-perpetuating nature of the stress reaction, you can see what happens. If you are someone who gets upset very easily, as time goes by, more and more of your thoughts will become negative. They will colour the way you see your life: your view of the world will become perpetually black; you'll see insult where none is offered and you'll expect the worst. You'll doubt yourself and your ability to cope. This will cause you even more stress and make your life much more difficult to control than if you had been born a calmer person. You will become prey to all the effects of stress outlined in the last chapter. By the same token, even if you are born with a reasonably placid nature, frequent upsetting experiences in adulthood can have a similar effect, though perhaps not as severe a one.

Having said all this, however, do not feel that you are doomed by either your heredity or your history. The techniques that you will learn in this book will still work for you whether you were born 'nervy' or 'a worrier' or whether life has been really unkind to you. Really exciting new research in the mind-body area shows that the changes in the way your brain operates that are brought about by childhood stress can be reversed. Therapy and self-help, if effective, produce physical changes in the brain.

> *Your heredity and history can be overcome. Therapy and self-help can produce changes in the brain.*

Creating an easily stressed brain

What are some of the typical ways in which an easily stressed brain is created? And what are their effects on your life? It is a paradox that while wanting our children to do well, we sometimes set up the conditions that will prevent that. Some of the ways in which parents bring up their children, the techniques they use to socialise them and make them good citizens, can make you more vulnerable to stress in your later life. Some child-rearing methods are very stressful for children; without realising it, you can make your children into helpless victims. But the effects don't stop once you grow up and start to run your own life. Helplessness in childhood produces a less resilient and a less coping adult. You can believe in your helplessness so that even when circumstances change and you are able to take control, you won't try.

> *Some of the ways you are brought up can make you more vulnerable to stress in later life.*

A single major traumatic incident in a child's life, or also in an adult life, can produce an adult who is less resistant to stress. Like a boulder hurled into a still pond, the ripples spread out to disturb your entire life. Any situation of extreme stress in which your life has been strongly out of your control can leave you sensitised, fragile and raw, and unsure of your ability to manage your life in the future. The crippling effects are the same whether you have endured a long period of stress or a brief but intense episode; only their severity may vary.

> *A major traumatic incident, as a child or adult, can make you less resistant to stress.*

Victims of emotional abuse

The most common cause of increased vulnerability to stress as an adult is a history of emotional abuse as a child. What is emotional abuse? Most dictionaries do not have a definition of emotional abuse; research on the topic is still in its early stages. If someone is being emotionally abusive to you, they criticise you, they put you down, they humiliate you and they blame you for everything; nothing is their fault, it's always yours. If the abuse is extreme, they break their promises to you, they lie and their criticism goes beyond disapproval to deliberately inflicting pain and suffering on you. The effects of emotional abuse on your thinking, your emotions and your behaviour are most damaging.

> *The most common cause of increased vulnerability to stress as an adult is a history of emotional abuse as a child.*

Many people in Western countries are exposed to the milder forms of emotional abuse because in a great number of countries, emotional abuse is the preferred way of socialising children, although of course it's not seen as abusive by those who use it. In England, Australia and New Zealand, for example, the tendency to bring up your children by criticising them for the things that they do wrong but never praising them for the things they do right has been a predominant way of child-rearing. Both parents and teachers may do it. It's supposed to make children modest and know their place – you don't want to bring up kids who are 'too big for their boots', 'swollen headed' or 'arrogant'. In New Zealand, there is even a special word for the person who is not appropriately modest. It's 'skite'. No parent in their right mind would want their child to be a 'skite'.

Unfortunately, instead of producing an adult who is unassuming but secure, what you do by criticising and never praising your children is to produce an individual who is unconfident, insecure and less well equipped to cope with stress. Criticism cripples children. It makes them doubt themselves and it lowers their self-esteem both in their early years and often as adults. You grow up knowing all your faults but none of your strengths. You grow up believing nothing you do is right.

Of course, not all parents or teachers are like this, certainly fewer now than in the 1950s or 1960s when there were no courses on positive parenting and few adequate books on child-rearing and self-esteem, but emotional abuse is still all too common. If you have experienced it in an extreme form, it is an enormous liability; it produces long-term vulnerability to stress and it does this in a number of ways. The way in which you, an individual, are affected may not be exactly the same as your neighbour – or your brother or sister – but you will be left with some or all of the following after-effects.

> *Criticism, put-downs, blaming and broken promises produce a person who is unconfident, insecure and less well equipped to cope with stress.*

The damage of emotional abuse

A torn jacket is soon mended;
But hard words bruise the heart of a child.
HENRY WADSWORTH LONGFELLOW

Poor self-esteem

If you have been blamed, criticised and put down over a long period, whether as a child or as an adult, you will doubt yourself. Even if you know that you're not always in the wrong, and that not everybody thinks you're naughty, useless, hopeless and bad, if someone says it often enough to you – particularly someone in a position of power, trust or responsibility – no matter what you say to yourself instead, you do come to believe it. You will see yourself as someone who never gets it right, someone who is a victim in the world, someone who is powerless.

I think I've always been insecure, since I was a kid really. My parents were very distant and very critical. They didn't talk to me about anything and they made me feel anything I did was wrong. I remember my mother never told me about sex. When I got my period she just gave me some sanitary towels and told me to read the packet. I was too scared to ask anyone what to do. I had no friends at school. I hated it at school, I didn't think that I fitted in. I didn't like the way I looked; that was partly my parents too. They were very judgemental and down-putting about my looks. When I was 14, I decided that I needed to lose some weight and I started throwing up. I think I'm probably still pretty close to anorexia; I haven't had periods for three years, but they have been coming and going really since I was 15.

If you have poor self-esteem as a child, it is likely to continue on into adulthood, whether you're still the victim of criticism and put-downs or not. It is surprising how many of our top achievers – politicians, managers, professionals and artists – are still in their heads the dumb, useless, unattractive, unpopular children they thought they were when their self-concept was first formed. Though these qualities bear no relationship to your later adult achievements, they tend to stick with you. You never question whether they are still true, or indeed whether they ever were true. They probably bore no relationship to your childhood or adolescent achievements either, but because you heard them repeatedly, you believed them and they became your reality.

> *If you have poor self-esteem as a child, it is likely to continue into adulthood.*

Perfectionism

Of course, criticism may motivate you to do well, but if you've been criticised without being praised or if you've always been told that you could do better, you'll still doubt yourself, and at best you're likely to be anxious and a perfectionist. As a child you may have needed to get things right to escape the criticism, but as an adult getting things right becomes a habitual way of dealing with the world. You can become obsessed with meeting deadlines, doing the perfect job and doing things the right way.

Perfectionists can be very difficult to live with, or to work for. They are very rigid; everything has to be done the way they want it. They are also often their own worst enemies. If things aren't 'just so' they become stressed and upset; they are often angry with themselves and others. Perfectionism can also stop you reaching your full potential. You may paralyse yourself if you're a perfectionist. When everything has to be exactly right, taking on new tasks may become a monumental effort.

I simply cannot leave the house in the morning unless all the housework's done. The beds have to be made, the floors and dishes done and the washing hung out. I feel anxious and guilty if anything's out of place. I suppose it's the influence of my upbringing – my mother was really strict on being tidy. She'd come sweeping through the house if you had your toys out and tidy them away while you were playing with them. I'd love to get a job now my children are in school, but I don't think I'd ever be able to get there on time because of the housework.

> Trying to be perfect is a way for a child to escape criticism, but as an adult it can become a habitual way of dealing with the world.

Anxiety and lack of trust

If, as a child, you're frequently criticised for the things you do and the way you do them, instead of becoming a perfectionist or becoming helpless you may end up a worrier, constantly anxious about doing the right thing. As a child you will be more easily stressed, and like the other effects of emotional abuse, this anxiety continues on into your adulthood. When the criticism and the control of your childhood has gone, you will still look at the world apprehensively. The universe has become a place in which bad things happen. It is difficult for you to see it as a benevolent place or to trust the human beings who inhabit it to treat you well.

I'm someone who is preoccupied with failure. I can't handle new situations – if I'm not prepared, I go into panic mode. If I have to do a presentation for work, I can't eat the day before, I can't sleep the night before and I generally have diarrhoea on the morning of it. I've always thought I wasn't good enough, that I didn't make the grade and I've always striven to please my parents, but I've never been able to.

> Constant criticism as a child can make you anxious, always worried about doing the right thing.

Abusive relationships with your partners and friends

If you believed you were worthless as a child, you are more likely, as an adult, to get into emotionally or physically abusive relationships. If your partner starts to criticise you and to put you down, you won't say, 'Hey, where do you get off, speaking to me like that', you will believe you deserve it; it will seem like normality; you may even accept it and not notice that it's happening.

I was totally unaware of myself for 17 years. I went through a period of bad depression and they said, 'Your life must be going wrong.' I said, 'There's nothing wrong with my life.' I was so used to making things right for everyone else. If we got through the day and everything was done, it was an OK day; I never thought of my own needs. People used to say, 'He puts you down constantly', and I didn't even notice it.

Don't think that if you put up with emotional abuse, your abuser will stop dishing it out. They won't; you will continue to receive even more of it. The movie *Thelma and Louise* has a great line that puts this more succinctly: 'You get what you accept'.

> *If you felt worthless as a child, you are more likely, as an adult, to get into relationships where you suffer emotional or physical abuse.*

Vulnerability to creating stress

Being a victim of emotional abuse not only makes you more vulnerable to experiencing stress but it also makes you more vulnerable to creating stress in your life. Unfortunately, many of the lessons of our childhood are learned unconsciously. If you've been emotionally abused as a child, even though you didn't like the abuse, you're more likely to become an emotional abuser yourself. That is not too difficult to understand when you look at the fact that, by and large, most people grow up to do the things that they were taught in childhood. Those who emotionally abused you didn't deliberately intend you to grow up being critical, martyr-like and defensive. You probably shouldn't blame them – chances are high that their childhood was emotionally abusive too and they learned no other way of socialising you. Even though you did not like their treatment of you, you may not recognise that you do it in your own intimate relationships.

> *Being a victim of emotional abuse makes you more vulnerable to experiencing and creating stress.*

If you do behave in this way, you will create more stress for yourself – you won't have good relationships with your friends or your partners. Your friends won't be there for the long haul; your partner may stick around a bit longer, but it won't be permanent. In the beginning they may do what you want, but at the same time you systematically destroy their self-confidence. Continually criticising them and putting them in the wrong makes them feel inadequate and self-doubting. In the early days your partner may believe that everything is their fault and if they just behave differently and be more what you want them to be, things will come right. In the long run they often come to see that things can't always be their fault, they can't always be in the wrong. Partners become aware that not everybody thinks they are worthless or treats them like you do. Eventually their love turns to resentment, and their willingness to please you, to hostility – and your relationship breaks up.

> I can't stand living with him anymore. He goes on like a raving lunatic. I was going to watch something on television and he said he wanted his clothes washed. I said, 'I'll do it after I've seen this program,' and he said, 'Do it now or I'll smack you one.' He's always threatening me and he makes me feel guilty all the time, and then he says it's just my interpretation of things. He says everything is my fault and tells me I'm deranged. He says to the kids that I'm mental. He's always right – he's even like that at work. He insists that there is absolutely nothing wrong with him. He is really just like his father; that's how his father is to his mother. His anger is extreme. He has never actually touched me but I am scared of him. He threatens me all the time and sometimes he really loses it. I have lost all my confidence over the years and I worry all the time.

Abusive relationships with your children

> Children begin by loving their parents. After a time they judge them.
> Rarely, if ever, do they forgive them.
>
> OSCAR WILDE

If you have children and you use emotional abuse to socialise them, you won't produce the child you want. Most parents want their children to be independent, happy, outgoing and achieving, but these are not the children you will rear if you're continually criticising, putting down, blaming and humiliating them. You will end up feeling cheated and unhappy about the way your children have turned out. In later years, in adolescence and after they have left home, your relationships with your children will not be close. They may be either uncomfortable and unconfident with you, or they may dislike you.

You're not doomed to repeat the cycle, though. If you can see what happened to you, it is possible to stand outside it and say to yourself, 'I'm not going to do that to the people I love. I will not tear them down. I will support, encourage and praise them.'

It's not only emotional abuse as a child that will make you more vulnerable to stress, sometimes you're unlucky enough to be physically abused as well. Although many parents are verbally abusive without being physically abusive, the reverse is not true. Rarely do you get physical abuse on its own. It is generally accompanied by emotional abuse. Parents who control their children through physical punishment commonly use both verbal and physical means of abuse.

There is a distinction between discipline and abuse. Many parents smack their children for misdemeanours when they consider them too young to be reasoned with. This is not necessarily abuse, though there are more effective ways of teaching children than hitting them. But if you thought the physical punishment you received as a child was unfair, or if you were afraid of the person who delivered it, it was abusive.

Victims of physical violence

We are effectively destroying ourselves by
Violence masquerading as love.

R. D. LAING

You may be surprised to know that everything in this section applies to you just as strongly if you were not physically abused yourself but witnessed the physical abuse of someone else – your mother or your siblings. You can learn the messages of fear and power and control just as readily by seeing someone else made the victim of violence as by experiencing it yourself.

Generally parents who physically punish their children want them to behave well. If the children don't behave, they hit them. They genuinely believe this is the best way to teach children what is correct behaviour. But is it? In fact, physical abuse is not particularly effective as a teaching method, and, like emotional abuse, if you're a victim of it, it seriously compromises your ability to withstand stress both as a child and as an adult. The evidence for this is overwhelming.

> *Physical abuse as a child seriously affects your ability to withstand stress, as a child and as an adult.*

The sad thing about physical abuse is that it doesn't usually stop children doing what adults disapprove of for long, or they wouldn't have to continue using it. And if it does teach children to refrain from doing what they're being hit for, it also teaches them many other things that aren't helpful in the long run, like, 'It's okay to hit the weak ... Might is right ... Losing your temper gets you what you want ... Other people's feelings don't matter.'

Many studies have shown that children who experience physical abuse or who witness it in their homes do less well academically, get on less well with their teachers and have fewer friends while they are at school. As adults, they are less likely to be employed, they have poorer relationships with other people, they are more likely to be depressed, to spend time in mental health facilities and more likely to come into conflict with the law. They may themselves grow up to be violent or victims of violence. How does this come about?

The effects of physical violence

Fear, anxiety, lack of trust

Physical abuse is painful and children are frightened of those who inflict hurt upon them or whom they see inflicting it on others. Whether you tell your child, 'This hurts me more than it hurts you' ... 'I'm doing this for your own good' ... 'I'm only doing this because I love you', or whether you don't, your child will still experience fear and anxiety at the thought of being hit, and suffer severe stress while being bit. Even in the times when you are not actively violent, anxiety and fear may permeate your home. Where abuse is frequent and extreme, children may also experience learned helplessness: they learn that they are not in control of their lives – you are.

I was so scared of my parents when I was a kid that I used to sit at the table and shake and hope that they wouldn't ask me anything. I could never eat my dinner and of course that just made them pick on me more. I remember when I was a really little child, probably before I was at school, if I went near anything, Mum would hit me to teach me not to touch things that weren't mine. I think they only ever saw the bad things about me, especially Dad. When I was at high school I wanted to do things and they wouldn't let me. The thrashings got really bad; I couldn't stand it anymore, and when I was 15 I had a breakdown.

The effects of physical abuse are very similar to those of emotional abuse, only they are normally more severe and longer lasting. If you have been physically mistreated, or witnessed others being hurt, you have been doubly victimised. In addition to the legacy of poor self-esteem, missed opportunities, stunted potential, abusive relationships, anxiety, lack of trust, you're likely to be left with problems to do with aggression as well.

You're more likely to put up with violence in your relationships if you have been physically abused as a child, or witnessed it, particularly if you're a woman. Research shows that many battered women, women who live in situations of domestic violence, have been abused as children or have seen their mother become a victim of their father's or stepfather's violence. For these women, violence is a more accepted way of life than it is for people who have never experienced it as children. It's not liked, but it's often seen as an inevitable part of the way in which human beings interact.

> *The effects of physical abuse are very similar to those of emotional abuse, but are normally more severe and longer lasting.*

Anger problems

> *A man in a passion rides a horse that runs away with him.*
>
> THOMAS FULLER

The cycle of violence is as self-perpetuating as the cycle of emotional abuse. Violence can be used as a stress-release mechanism. You're more likely to be angry if you're worried or upset about something, because when you're stressed every emotion is intensified. If you blow your top and get physically violent it does release some of the tension. It gets rid of some of the stored-up energy that's seething inside your body; it's the fight/flight mechanism at work. Your body actually feels more physically relaxed after you've been violent. If you're more vulnerable to stress because you've been a victim of physical assault or you had a parent who has set you the example of violence, when you're really under pressure and not totally rational, you tend to revert to that first example as a way of releasing your stress.

Giving rein to your anger can lead to many problems. Like emotional abuse, a background of physical abuse makes you more susceptible, not only to experiencing stress, but to creating it for yourself in your life. If you cannot control your physical anger, you're likely to end up with problems with the law. This is more common if you're male but it also happens to women.

> *You're more likely to be angry if you're anxious, because when you're stressed every emotion is intensified.*

Abusive relationships

It is probably in your close relationships that physical abuse will create most havoc in your life. If you have been exposed to violence in your childhood, you're more likely, unfortunately, to become aggressive and abusive in your relationships. This is true even if you didn't like what happened to you as a child, and even if you say to yourself, 'I won't do that in my own relationships.'

Men who have been mistreated as children or who have seen their fathers or stepfathers beat their mothers are not only more likely to physically abuse other men, including their friends, they are more likely to beat their female partners and their children. And it's not only men who have aggression problems. Although women victims of childhood violence are less likely than men who have been victims to be abusive to other adults, it is not unknown for this to happen. Women who are violent to their children and come before the courts have frequently been abused as children themselves.

I'm 36 years old and I'm still afraid of my father. He used to knock us around as kids and he still gets ugly-tempered and still tells me what to do. He was always bad-tempered when I was young and I was always terrified of him, but it was worse if he was drinking. He never talked to me. If I ever did anything wrong he would just shout at me and belt me and send me to my room. He never listened to what I said, he'd never ask for an explanation of what happened and if my sister and I were fighting it was always my fault. He did belt her, but never as much as he beat me up. Home was just a place that you wanted to be away from. He and Mum used to yell at each other too, and he would hit her as well. I have to admit, though I hate it, that I see certain similarities between us now. I'm aggressive and moody and I flare up a lot. It doesn't matter who it is, I just flare up with anyone, whether it's a friend or a stranger. It's cost me a lot of friendships.

Are you inevitably doomed to be violent if you were a victim of brutality? Studies have shown that not every adult who was physically abused as a child or who witnessed it will go on to mistreat their own partners and children. You can stop the cycle if you were a victim. Nevertheless, if you were a victim the dice are loaded against you. The vast majority of men who are violent to their partners and their children, and the vast majority of women who are violent to their children, were themselves exposed to violence as children.

> **If you have been exposed to violence in childhood, you're more likely to become aggressive and abusive in your relationships. You can stop the cycle, but it is difficult.**

Although violence has a short-term pay-off in that people may do what you want because they're scared not to, in the long run, being violent doesn't really improve your life. As with emotional abuse, your partner ends up not loving you but resenting you, and eventually being terrified of you. If you're physically abusive towards them, your children don't grow up the way you would probably like them to: in control of their own lives, confident and secure, but the reverse – they grow up just like you. For, if you are physically abusive, it's very unlikely that you will value yourself. Whether you're critical of your own violent behaviour or not, your earlier exposure to violence will still have sapped your confidence and made you less able to control your own life. You're likely to see yourself as a failure in some way.

Adult victims of violence

What happens if you're not a victim of violence as a child but as an adult? Like emotional abuse, if you are subjected to a physically abusive relationship after your childhood, damage will still be done but it may not be as severe. You will become more vulnerable to stress then and later in your life. The harm that's done by physical abuse is the same, no matter when in your life you become a victim, but, all other things being equal, physical violence in adulthood is likely to have less severe and enduring effects than if it happens to you as a child.

The legacy of violence is probably more long lasting if you were a child victim, because you may never have learned how to handle stress properly. You may never have learned to be confident that you do have strengths and good qualities, or learned how to have good relationships with other people. Taking control of your life is not a matter of regaining your confidence and your ability to handle your emotions; it's a matter of learning this from scratch. Taking control of your life is a more complicated process if you were physically abused as a child, but is possible.

> *Being physically abused as an adult will harm you, but it may not be as severe. You will become more vulnerable to stress then and later in your life.*

Victims of sexual abuse

Fear, anxiety, lack of trust

The long-term effects of sexual abuse are very similar to those of extreme emotional abuse and of physical abuse, and for the same reasons. If you are sexually abused, your life is out of your control and you become, to some degree, helpless. Even if it is not accompanied by physical pain, sexual abuse is frequently accompanied by extreme fear and powerlessness and great anxiety and stress. The effects of an experience like this are not short-lived: even when sexual abuse is discontinued, these effects live on. You are likely to be unconfident, to fail to reach your potential and to be vulnerable emotionally.

If you have been a victim of sexual abuse, you are far more susceptible to stress. You will get more emotional about everything that upsets you, but certain emotions are likely to predominate. Guilt is one of these; anger, fear and frustration are others.

When I was little I used to stay at my grandfather's on the weekends; my brother came too. My earliest memories are of not wanting to go. I used to cry not to go and remember being scared and terrified at night when I was there. My clear memories start when I was seven or eight. Then I remember that my grandfather used to come into the bedroom when I was asleep and he would sexually abuse me. I remember not wanting to go to sleep – I was scared to go to sleep. I could hear him coming down the hall every night. I couldn't tell anyone what he was doing to me. I knew it was wrong, but I thought it must be my fault. I was scared that no-one would believe me because I was a kid and he was a grown-up. Also I knew that Mum really liked him and looked up to him. I felt it was my fault – it must be something that I was doing wrong, because this happened to me. I think it's had a bad effect on me. I was always depressed – it's been as long as I can remember, ever since I was a kid, and I still think everything's my fault. Eighteen months ago I felt that I was suicidal, but I couldn't put my finger on anything that was wrong. It has made me hate myself; I'm always telling myself that I'm a jerk. I wish I was able to have a more interesting life and have some friends. I don't seem to be interested in anything. I haven't got any hobbies. I'm flatting with three other people but I don't really get on with them. I'm a bit afraid of them, actually. I'm also quite afraid of doing things wrong at work.

If you have been sexually abused, no matter how much you know intellectually that you didn't initiate it or want the abuse to happen, you're still vulnerable to thoughts such as: 'Was it my fault? ... Did I ask for it? ... Did I deserve it? ... Wasn't there something I could have done to stop it?' The answer to all these questions is an emphatic No, but the questions persist, making you more susceptible to guilt from all sources, robbing you of confidence and increasing your self-doubt.

Feelings of anger and frustration after being sexually abused arise from the powerlessness of being a victim, from having had no control over something that is not only frightening or terrifying but often painful, revolting and humiliating to you.

> *The effects of sexual abuse continue long after the abuse stops: anxiety, stress, lack of confidence and emotional fragility.*

Relationship problems

You often lose your faith in other human beings if you've been a sexual abuse victim, because more often than not, you are abused by someone known to you. An adult you should have been able to trust has abused that trust. Difficulties with relationships are common after sexual abuse for a number of reasons: you may feel you can't rely on anyone, so commitment to any one person or relationship becomes difficult for you; because you lack confidence and get upset easily, you often feel insecure and jealous in relationships.

> *I'm really insecure in my relationships. I go to pieces if my partner needs time by himself – I feel that it's all directed at me and I get really jealous. I find it hard to believe that someone loves me and I am always testing them. I've never believed that anybody liked me or loved me, because I think my parents didn't. Dad sexually abused me and I believe my mother knew about it and did nothing. It's made it hard for me to have good friendships and to believe what people say to me. I hate talking to people about myself and I just can't accept compliments.*

> **Difficulties with relationships are common after sexual abuse.**

Sexual problems

After being abused, you may also find difficulties around your sexuality. When you're introduced to sex in an inappropriate or negative way, it's often hard to make a so-called normal adjustment. Sexual problems after sexual abuse are varied. You may find that sex is off-putting to you and that you're scared of sexual relationships, or that you're not very easily aroused sexually. You may be phobic about certain sexual activities. Sex can be fine until your partner does one of the things that your abuser used to do, which makes you freeze up entirely and all the old panicky feelings start to flood back.

> *I always think people are getting at me, I feel rejected a lot and I have this big problem with sex. I'm impotent a lot of the time. I think it's because of the way I first found out about sex. I was sexually abused when I was 12 years old. I feel terrible about it and it's something that I think about every day. It makes me feel that I'm different from other people, and I worry a lot about how I come across and about impressing people. It has a big effect on my relationships too. I'm really jealous. I'm jealous even when things are okay sexually, but if they are not, then I am just super jealous. I don't think I trust*

anybody really, certainly not my girlfriends. I don't like people to get too close to me, they can't hurt you then.

At the other end of the spectrum, after experiencing sexual abuse you may feel that sex is no big deal and you wonder why people place all this importance upon it. You think, 'Oh well, if they want it, why not', or you automatically assume that for a partner to care about you, sex has to be part of any relationship, and so you become what is labelled promiscuous. It is estimated that a majority of women who become prostitutes have been sexually abused earlier in their lives.

> **When you're introduced to sex in an inappropriate or negative way, it's often hard to adjust to normal relationships.**

Sexual deviance

Perhaps the most damaging effects of sexual abuse are where it becomes self-perpetuating: where the victim of abuse later becomes the abuser. This happens far more frequently with men, but the reality is that it also happens with women.

It's not inevitable that if you are male and you have been sexually abused you will go on to abuse others yourself. The mechanisms by which this happens are being researched now. Whether you go on to abuse other people depends in a major way upon your sexual fantasies. Sexual fantasies are the thoughts and scenarios you use to get yourself sexually aroused. They are what you think of when you're masturbating or having sex or just thinking sexual thoughts to yourself. If your sexual fantasies or thoughts involve sexually abusing others, whether it's forcing others to have sex with you or whether it's having sex with children, or any other of the forms that sexual abuse takes, chances are very strong that ultimately you'll act these out and become sexually abusive yourself. It is particularly likely if your only sexual fantasy is an abusive one. If you're worried about whether you're vulnerable in this way, ask yourself whether what you fantasise about is illegal in the eyes of the law. If it is, you are at risk and you should consult a therapist.

Therapy for sexual deviance is possible, but it needs to be therapy carried out by someone skilled in the treatment of sexual deviance. You wouldn't want to try to change this for yourself or go to an untrained amateur. The odds of failing are too high and the costs are profound. Where sexual abuse has caused you to become an abuser, your potential for creating stress is enormous: you will have major problems with your relationships, you have the potential to destroy the lives of others, your own life will certainly be very difficult to control, and you may end up in prison.

> *Where sexual abuse has caused you to become an abuser,*
> *your potential for creating stress is great.*

Sexual abuse in adulthood

Sexual abuse in adulthood, like physical abuse and emotional abuse in adulthood, also has the same kinds of effects as sexual abuse in childhood; it predisposes you both to experiencing stress more strongly and to creating more stress for yourself. As with physical and emotional abuse, if you are a victim of sexual abuse as an adult, the effects can be less crippling. This is because you may have had a period in which your life was under control and in which you had confidence and the skills to manage your stress well. If you are sexually abused in childhood, it is unlikely that you would have ever had this. These are skills you will have to learn.

Victims of trauma: learned helplessness

Emotional, physical and sexual abuse are probably the most common causes of extreme vulnerability to stress in later life, but there are other experiences which can damage you and sensitise you to over-reacting to stress later. Any single extremely traumatic event can leave you a changed person, weakening your ability to cope with later stress and destroying your confidence in yourself and your belief in your ability to control your life. Why is this? What are the similarities between the various forms of abuse and traumatic experiences? Is there some underlying mechanism at work here?

> *Any extremely traumatic event can weaken your ability*
> *to cope with later stress and destroy your confidence.*

Incidents causing learned helplessness

The kind of traumatic events that leave you with extreme vulnerability to stress are usually those where you experience profound fear and no control. They are generally incidents where your life is on the line, where you genuinely believe that you may die or be physically harmed. They can also be situations in which you witness someone else die or be seriously harmed. They are situations that cause learned helplessness – that paralysis of the will brought about by a condition of extreme stress. When the stress in a particular situation is so great that your efforts at controlling it repeatedly come to nothing, you not only stop trying to control that situation, you may also give up trying to control some new situations.

Victims of physical abuse and sexual abuse can suffer learned helplessness, and victims of severe emotional abuse can also. People caught in life-threatening situations like earthquakes, wars, airline disasters, hostage situations, major car accidents, and the like, may do so as well. Learned helplessness itself is a direct result of the stress reaction. It is an inevitable consequence of the way the human body is constructed. Given the requisite circumstances, you will experience it. What are these circumstances?

Events where you experience great fear and no control are likely to leave you with extreme vulnerability to stress. Learned helplessness is a direct result of the stress reaction.

Experiencing learned helplessness

Remember the effects of the stress chemicals on the brain? They impair concentration and memory and produce an inability to think clearly or to make rational decisions. They do this by interfering with the effects of the chemicals responsible for neural transmission, the brain's information processing.

Once you believe that you are helpless, you become helpless.

When the stress reaction has kept you at high levels of arousal over a long period, as it does with physical, sexual or extreme emotional abuse, or where it has occurred very intensely in a terrifying situation – as it may, for example, if you're held hostage and believe you could die if you're under fire in a war; or if you're trapped in a car, can smell the petrol leaking and believe you won't get out alive – you can't think rationally, and you come to believe it is impossible to escape your situation.

Post-traumatic stress disorder

Learned helplessness has long-term effects that are responsible for you becoming more vulnerable to stress later on. The effect of a trauma that is sufficient to cause learned helplessness does not disappear rapidly or easily, even when the victim is removed from the situation. The symptoms that remain are known as post-traumatic stress disorder and they may last for a long period, sometimes for the rest of the victim's life.

Post-traumatic stress disorder is not a new term. It was coined after the Vietnam War when soldiers returning from the front were unable to fit into society again. Soldiers who had been terrified under fire, and had felt helpless then, adjusted to civilian life differently from others. Many became suicidal or homicidal, some were unable to work; they suffered nightmares, phobias and panic attacks. If they heard a car backfire, they dived for cover in fear. Their marriages broke up and they failed in their new relationships.

The same set of symptoms was observed in servicemen coming back from the First and Second World Wars, but then it was labelled shell shock. In fact, post-traumatic stress disorder has been around for as long as human beings have. It is caused by being in a situation of profound and uncontrollable fear, helplessness or horror and being unable to remove oneself from this situation. In addition to low confidence and vulnerability to stress, if you have post-traumatic stress disorder, you may also have other symptoms that puzzle you. The disorder is characterised by a re-experiencing of the traumatic event. Commonly you will have frequent painful thoughts about what happened to you, or frequent dreams or nightmares in which you re-experience the original cause of your stress, whether it is physical abuse, sexual abuse or a one-time terrifying experience.

You may also have flashbacks: physical feelings of panic triggered off by events that remind you of the original cause of your stress. These are often quite bewildering. You wonder where they come from. If you were raped in an elevator, you may break out in a sweat every time you get into an elevator. If you were beaten severely as a child, you may tremble and cry at raised voices.

Since I got raped, I'm like a totally different person. I've made a lot of enemies, I get depressed all the time and I'm restless and I feel aggro. I feel I'm a nobody. I can't sleep, even when somebody else is in the house. If I do sleep, I have these shocking dreams, sometimes they're about the rape, but sometimes they are about other terrible things. I'm always waking up either paralysed with fear or crying. I can't concentrate on school; I get into fights. There are lots of things I can't do anymore. I can't have a shower if there is nobody in the house, and I have to lock the door even when there is. If I try to go in when no-one else is home, I start panting and my heart goes flat out, because the rape was in the bathroom. I also feel sick and sweat whenever anybody talks about rape too.

Post-traumatic stress disorder is also characterised by other symptoms, among them fears, sleep disturbances, memory problems, the inability to concentrate, and anxiety. In short, it is characterised by a far greater susceptibility to stress – you can recognise these now as stress symptoms.

Some occupations are more likely to expose you to incidents that will result in post-traumatic stress. Being a soldier is one of these, but then so is being a taxi driver. In the United States, taxi drivers are more likely to die violent deaths than police, but police officers and prison officers too have their share of situations in which they suffer uncontrollable fear and are left with post-traumatic stress.

Post-traumatic stress disorder is a very intense form of vulnerability to later stress and it has some special features that other forms of vulnerability don't have, in particular the obsessive thoughts, the nightmares and the flashbacks. Nevertheless, the kinds of after-effects of a childhood where you were controlled through emotional abuse are the same in nature, only less intense in severity.

> *Post-traumatic stress disorder is caused by being in a situation of profound and uncontrollable fear, helplessness or horror and being unable to remove yourself from this situation.*
> *It is characterised by a far greater susceptibility to stress.*

The effects of trauma

A reasonably brief period of extreme stress as a child or an adult – for example, a broken relationship or the death of someone close to you – can have some of the same effects as those of trauma and abuse. You may feel the old certitudes and assurances you had are gone; you can't trust the world or your ability to control it any longer. You are left over-sensitive to stress and doubtful about your ability to run your life as you want to.

The effects of non-life-threatening periods of trauma on your later vulnerability to stress are different only in severity from those that cause post-traumatic stress disorder; they are not really very different in kind. One of the reasons for this similarity is likely to be the changes in your thinking that are brought about by living through a prolonged period of stress. Recall the effects of the stress chemicals on your brain – they produce depressed, paranoid, pessimistic thinking. This way of thinking can become predominant. Not only are you more vulnerable to over-reacting to stress when it happens to you, you become more vulnerable to creating it for yourself. You don't expect things to work out well for you, you don't expect to succeed. You see the half empty glass, rather than the half full. You become a pessimist about life, rather than an optimist. You may say, 'What's wrong with being a pessimist – at least you're never disappointed.' In fact, you are probably permanently disappointed.

Researchers Michael Scheier and Charles Carver, in the United States, have looked at the effects of this way of thinking in their studies of optimists and pessimists. Their research is covered more fully in Chapter 4, but their conclusions are unequivocal: it is not good to be a pessimist. Pessimists are less healthy psychologically and physically. They experience life as harder and less manageable, and they are more likely to avoid dealing with problems or to give up on attempts to solve them.

If, from your reading of this chapter, you have identified yourself as suffering from the after-effects of earlier stress, or of being someone who is more susceptible to stress than other people, or if you have identified your child as having been through a situation which has made him or her vulnerable to stress, don't feel you or they are condemned to a lifetime of being this way. You can still learn the ways to keep yourself calm and positive, to identify and deal with your stress and to regain your confidence and create a fulfilling life.

If you have been the victim of sexual abuse or extreme violence, you may need to see a trained professional in order to be able to attain an attitude to your abuse that you can live with. There are some techniques mentioned in later chapters which, when used by competent therapists, can eliminate the effects of trauma for good. If you have particular fears and phobias around sexual activity or if you suspect that you may abuse someone yourself, you should definitely see a therapist who is trained to deal with dysfunctional sexual behaviour, because you are unlikely to know the specific techniques that will help you. Regardless of that, the techniques that are taught in this book will help you to make today and tomorrow positive and rewarding and they will help you to put the past behind you.

> *The effects of non-life-threatening trauma on your later vulnerability to stress are often similar to post-traumatic stress disorder, but not as severe. But you can deal with your stress and regain your confidence.*

Summing Up

- Do not fear knowing your liabilities, both genetic and learned; they can be overcome.
- Identify your biological barriers to achieving your full potential.
- Learn what life experiences may leave you a legacy of unhappiness.
- Find out why you may not be as confident, as relaxed or as successful in your relationships as you want to be.
- Discover that you can break out of this cycle.

Recognising the many guises of stress

Man who man would be
Must rule the empire of himself.

P. B. SHELLEY

Put out the sparks and prevent the fire

In Chapter 1 you learned about the pernicious, self-propagating nature of stress: how it runs through your life like a forest fire, distorting your thoughts, emotions, behaviour and physical functions. Sometimes the recognition that you are stressed comes too late for you to fight your way out of the blackened, smouldering mess that you have created. The relationship that died and left you feeling shattered for years might never have burned out if you'd noticed the distress flares earlier. Even more devastatingly, the stroke or heart attack which cuts you down in your sixties might have been averted if you'd recognised the warning signs in your twenties.

*It is vital that you recognise the signs of stress as
early as possible in order to stabilise your life before
it gets beyond control.*

Early identification of your individual symptoms of stress is the best strategy for
ensuring the longest and happiest life possible. This means attuning yourself to
often subtle changes in your mind and your body. When an event disturbs you,
it vibrates like a seismic tremor through every aspect of your life. Sometimes
the evident damage is the equivalent of a skyscraper collapsing, but more often
the effects of the tremor are at first hardly visible on the surface; a barely
discernible shift has taken place, which nevertheless affects all of the following:

1. Your thinking
2. Your emotions
3. The way your body feels physically
4. The way your body functions and the efficiency with which it operates
5. The way you behave

These changes are all symptoms of stress. They are telling you that your
happiness is at risk and your life is verging on the uncontrollable. Sometimes
you notice one or two of these indicators and realise that you are stressed,
but it is not easy to recognise them at all five levels. Nonetheless, they will all
be there.

Identify negative thinking

Aim to identify the first stage of the cycle: the negative thinking which ignites
the stress cycle and allows stress to flourish. If you can accomplish that, you
have a good chance of easily reordering your life. However, it is better that you
identify any of the symptoms than none at all. If you recognise in yourself later
stages of stress such as behavioural or physical changes, you can learn to look
for the earlier indications.

*Try to identify the first stage of the cycle: the negative thinking
which ignites the stress cycle and allows stress to flourish.*

Perhaps you have become alarmed to find that your usually placid, friendly self has been replaced by a creature driven by outbursts of rage. Your inability to find a quick parking space at the shopping mall drives you into a frenzy; you thunder at your son for misplacing his shoes – and each of these events is accompanied by physical reactions such as a pounding heart and tense muscles. It is possible to trace these symptoms back to feelings of irritability and frustration, and ultimately to the thoughts which provoke your anger.

Often it is difficult to be objective about yourself, especially if you have entered a cycle where you have become entirely reactive – taking everything personally – but if you don't recognise that you are stressed, you cannot even begin to take control. The stories that follow are pieces of other people's lives that may help you to recognise stress symptoms of your own. Their characters all fail to recognise their stress or all misidentify its causes.

> *Recognising that you are stressed is the first step to taking control.*

Recognising thoughts

Paul sat down stiffly in his chair, flicking invisible dust from his sleeve. He was 46, tall, slim and well-groomed, wearing the expensive dark suit of a successful businessman. Although he sat very still, his eyes darted around the room and the muscles at the corners of his mouth showed white with tension.

Paul was the financial controller of his company, a multinational whose head office was in Boston. The company was not doing well, but although Paul was naturally concerned about its losses, the rational part of his brain understood that the situation was only temporary and that finances would improve in the coming year.

Paul, however, was not in a rational frame of mind. He was due to make his first trip to Head Office to discuss the financial condition of the company and could think of nothing else day and night. He was well aware that he was stressed. Folding his arms tightly across his chest, he said:

I feel like I'm going mad or something. I'm so obsessed with the thought of going to Boston, I can't carry out my normal work. I'm falling behind, not only with the preparations for my trip but with my day-to-day responsibilities. It shouldn't be like this. There's no reason for it! I know I've done my job well and it's not my fault we're not meeting budget.

Tormenting himself with the conviction that the trip would result in failure and humiliation, Paul's dark thoughts multiplied into a catalogue of disaster. He would be held to account for mismanagement of the company's finances. His explanations would be dismissed. He would lose his job. He'd never find another one. His marriage would collapse.

Further discussions revealed that Paul suffered from all the categories of stress. His thoughts about his trip were entirely negative. Emotionally, he felt constantly anxious. When he had to meet deadlines at work, this anxiety bordered on panic. He was attacked by physical symptoms. His heart raced, his headaches were frequent and his stomach felt 'like a whole barrow load of butterflies were in there'. In protest at the burden of stress, his body had begun to break down. He wasn't sleeping well, woke most mornings with griping diarrhoea and his doctor had told him that his blood pressure was up.

Paul had also noticed other changes in his behaviour. He said:

I'm having difficulty leaving home in the morning. I can't face going to work and I can't bring myself to drive on the motorway because it makes me feel even more panicky and out of control. I went to the movies with my wife last weekend and I couldn't stand the crowds in there. I really thought I'd suffocate. I had to leave the theatre. Everything frightens me! Even things that I know to be totally improbable, like the house burning down or my wife having an accident.

Because of the nature of the stress cycle, it is very common for unreasonable fears and even phobias to arise once anxiety has got a grip on your mind. The more you worry, the more stress chemicals pass through your brain, transmitting increasingly irrational, fearful thoughts.

Paul's story will appear again in the next five chapters. We'll follow his progress towards getting his life under control once more using the Five Step Life Plan.

Recognising emotions

> *There is a road from the eye to the heart*
> *That does not go through the intellect.*
>
> G. K. CHESTERTON

There are often moments when you know that you are moody or feeling dismal, that your emotions are in a turmoil, although you may not associate these bad feelings with stress. However, these sensations of unhappiness indicate that you are experiencing stress at the second stage of the cycle, at the level of your emotions. You recognise this most commonly when you are grieving, but stress may also be felt as other strong emotions.

> *Feelings of unhappiness may indicate you are experiencing stress at the level of your emotions.*

Antoinette didn't know she was stressed, and she didn't know what she was thinking, but she knew only too well what she was feeling. She was 30 years old, working as a doctor's receptionist. Efficient and friendly, she was popular with the other staff and patients. She lived with her boyfriend John. They had been together for three years and were planning to get married and start a family. To accelerate their savings program so that they could buy a house, John suggested that they invite Jillian, one of Antoinette's girlfriends, to share the house they were renting so they would have some extra income. Antoinette agreed to the arrangement and Jillian moved in. Then Antoinette's life began to fall apart.

Describing her situation in emotional terms, she said:

I feel jealous and insecure now Jillian is living with us. I'm constantly feeling either angry or depressed. I know it's stupid when I think about it, because John and I have a good relationship, but I just can't control the way I feel. It's wrecking my life and I'm becoming a person I hate.

Why would a woman like Antoinette feel jealous? Not only was she capable and popular at work, she also was very good-looking: tanned, blonde and apparently self-possessed. But jealousy has very little to do with external reality and a great deal to do with internal insecurity. Antoinette said she had felt insecure and jealous for most of her life but she had managed to suppress those emotions until she met John. Now that she was involved with a man she really loved, it seemed to her that she had a lot to lose if another woman should steal him away. When Jillian came to live with them, Antoinette's fears of loss and abandonment exploded into an out of control case of jealousy.

After much discussion Antoinette was able to identify the thoughts which triggered her feelings of jealousy and activated the rest of the stress cycle. She was thinking:

Jillian might come on to John. I know she's my friend, but that's no reason why she would be loyal to me. She might really resent me because I've got this great boyfriend. Did John suggest Jillian live here because he fancies her? Why should he care more about me than Jillian? She's much smarter than I am. I hate the way I look today. I wish I had hair like hers. John's probably tired of living alone with me because I'm so boring. He's probably having second thoughts about getting married to me now.

Antoinette also became aware that she was feeling constantly shaky and tearful. Her heart pounded, her stomach churned and her hands were clammy. Havelock Ellis described jealousy as 'that dragon that slays love under the pretence of keeping it alive'. Antoinette realised that she was in the process of killing off her relationship with John because of the way the stress of her jealousy had affected her behaviour. At work, as well as at home, she had become sulky, critical and angry and increasingly frightened by the alteration of her personality.

Recognising physical symptoms

The body never lies.

MARTHA GRAHAM

Identifying a state of stress as a purely emotional problem is not the only misjudgement you may make about stress. Sometimes, oblivious to the influence of your thoughts and feelings, you may mistake a physical stress symptom for the actual cause of your problems. All you know is that your body doesn't feel right. Your neck is stiff and your back aches, making it difficult to sit at your computer and concentrate on that project management report. You begin to fall behind in your work. One day you notice that your heart is thudding for no apparent reason. Straight away you begin to fret about illness and incapacity. You jump to extreme conclusions. You wonder if it's the first indication of a heart attack. You start to worry about who would look after the children if anything happened to you.

You've given up alcohol and caffeine and chocolate, but you're still plagued by unbearable headaches that stop you reading or watching television, which you used to do in order to relax. Or perhaps your body temperature has gone out of control. You regularly wake in the night so drenched in sweat you have to change the sheets on the bed; as a result, your partner has taken to sleeping in the spare room, which further estranges you from one another.

In these situations you are encountering stress at the third or fourth stage; the point at which stress is causing changes in the physical functioning of your body. Being out of touch with thoughts and feelings is a state that is particularly common in men because many males in Western cultures are sent a message from birth which says: 'Boys shouldn't have feelings, and if they do, they certainly shouldn't talk about them.' The myth of the strong, silent male, and the belief that 'big boys don't cry', are still alive and well, effectively preventing men from running their lives happily. Men, however, do not have a monopoly on this kind of alienation. It affects women too, especially those brought up to grin and bear life's adversities.

> *Our social conditioning means we are often out of touch with our thoughts and feelings.*

Prue was a small woman in her fifties, her sweet-looking face marked by fatigue. She said:

Mostly I can go to sleep all right, but come 2 a.m., or at the latest 4 a.m., and I'll wake up. Sometimes I'll go back to sleep for a couple of hours, but often I'll just doze till it's time to get up. It's really exhausting me and I'm not coping well in the day anymore.

While Prue was able to identify her insomnia as a physical symptom of stress, she insisted that she didn't feel mentally stressed and that her life was not difficult in any way, although it had been in the past. But since her doctor had been unable to find any physical reason for her sleeplessness, she was prepared to examine her thoughts, emotions and behaviour for a cause.

Her sleep problems had started nine months earlier when her husband had been involved in a car accident. A self-employed builder, his inability to work for six months had affected the whole family. Money was tight. A holiday planned for Prue and her granddaughter was cancelled and medical expenses had soaked up savings. Prue's husband, Bill, had found his invalid state very frustrating and the atmosphere in the house had been bleak and tense.

Three months previously, Bill had returned to work. Prue was unable to understand why she was still dogged by insomnia. 'After all,' she said, 'I held it together for that six months. I was cheerful and positive and supportive to Bill, but now that the worst is over I seem to have hit the wall.'

But when she looked more closely, Prue discovered that her stressed condition was triggered by thoughts that she described as confused and mixed up 'and not very nice'. These thoughts were accompanied by agitated emotions:

There were times when I got tired of Bill's complaining. I thought, well the accident happened – there's no use crying over spilt milk, we just have to get on with it. And I still think if he'd let me get medical insurance like I had wanted to, we wouldn't have had such a terrible time financially. And then I think I'm just as bad as him, complaining about what's in the past. And then I think, what's wrong with me? I'm not myself. I've never been one to let things get me down, but I've started to worry all the time about whether I'll get to sleep, and if I don't, will I be too tired to do all the things I have to?

Her emotions fluctuated between anxiety and depression and hopelessness.

Because Prue had always been a coper, changes in her behaviour were not marked. But when she really considered her actions, she admitted that she had found herself putting off household tasks, no longer experimenting with her cooking, avoiding her friends and making little effort to go out. Her stress caused her to reduce the scope of her life and her ability to find pleasure in the small things – an imaginative meal, a visit to the garden centre with a friend – which had once sustained her.

Recognising body breakdown

Health is not a condition of matter,
But of mind.

MARY BAKER EDDY

Some people are so disconnected from themselves that they are not able to perceive stress until their bodies actually begin to deteriorate and they realise something is amiss. Alterations in thoughts, emotions and bodily feelings are fairly obvious indications of a problematic state. But the failure of your body to function efficiently is less often recognised, even by doctors, as stress-related.

> *Your body's failure to function efficiently is less often recognised,*
> *even by doctors, as stress-related.*

This is stress in the aftermath of the fourth stage, that of physical changes to the body. Heart attacks, high blood pressure, asthma, eczema, rashes, dermatitis, migraines, headaches, irritable bowel, colitis and strokes are all strong signals that your life needs a serious overhaul. When stress has developed to this stage, it requires hard work to repair the damage, but the breakdown of the body must be seen as a cry for survival.

Graham, 52, sat blinking nervously on the couch with a mournful expression on his face. He had been referred to counselling by his doctor, who thought that he needed help to give up smoking and to control his weight, both of which were aggravating his persistent angina attacks. Until his doctor had suggested it, it had never occurred to Graham that he might be suffering from stress, although he described himself as a worrier. Graham sighed a great deal as he spoke.

I worry about my heart a lot of the time. It's on my mind off and on throughout the day, when I'm not worrying about other things in my life. I've been depressed at times in my life and got over it, but now I can't seem to make decisions. I think I've mucked my life up for a long time. My wife died of cancer years ago and I met another woman soon after, but she was married with young children and she didn't want to leave them. We were together for 10 years and I suppose that really stopped me from getting involved with anyone else. We drifted apart in the end and now I've met another woman. She moved in with me and I wish she wasn't there really. She's 10 years older than I am and very dogmatic. There are times when I tell her to go, but she won't, so I've just stopped arguing with her. I would like to have married someone who makes me happy.

Graham began to keep a diary of what was happening in his life. It soon became very clear to him that as well as his angina attacks, he had many of the earlier symptoms of stress, both physical and mental. He recorded thoughts and feelings that expressed the pervasive tension in his life.

Woke up with June on my mind. June not talking to me at breakfast table, feel uncomfortable, it's like that most mornings. June got angry because I didn't want to go to bingo. I feel frustrated and guilty. June came home from bingo and wouldn't talk to me. I felt frustrated and guilty. Next morning at breakfast time we didn't talk. I tried to talk. I feel very uneasy.

Graham saw that when he thought and felt like this, his palms began to sweat and his heart quickened. After the altercation over the bingo, he actually had an angina attack. His smoking and overeating were also related to his stress. Since June had moved in, he comforted himself with increasing numbers of cigarettes and snack foods. Other changes in his behaviour caused by his stress were less obvious, although he did become aware that he had lost enthusiasm for many of his former activities and had taken to slumping for hours in front of the TV.

Recognising changes in your behaviour

Anger is a kind of temporary madness.

ST BASIL

Sometimes you only become aware that you are stressed when your behaviour changes, when you start to act in ways that you know are out of character. A difficult customer walks into your store and you completely lose your cool when she complains about the service. You let fly with a stream of invective that is undignified and uncalled for. You single-handedly cause embarrassment and resentment and your day is ruined.

You are seething with frustration over what you consider to be the management inadequacies of your boss. Against all reason, you find yourself venting your spleen at him in a staff task force meeting, although aware, even as your tongue runs away with you, that you are revealing to your colleagues a lack of discipline and tact. At lunchtime, uncharacteristically, you go to a bar and miserably drink a double vodka while stewing over the fact that you have now alienated your boss and created a volatile situation at work that only doubles the pressure you feel you are under.

> *Changes in your behaviour show you are at the very end of the stress cycle.*

Behavioural changes such as these indicate a person at the very end of the stress cycle. When you are in this situation you often can't see how erratic your actions have become. It is the people around you who notice that your behaviour has degenerated. The effects of the stress chemicals on the brain blind you to objective judgement. You tend to blame your extreme reactions on the actions of others. Nothing is your fault; the whole world is against you. You see yourself as a helpless, but very angry, victim of awful circumstance.

Cindy, a supervisor in a clothing factory, was referred for counselling because her boss had received many complaints about her attitude. The women Cindy supervised objected to her aggressive manner and snappish tongue, Although Cindy was aware that she was reprimanding the staff more often than she used to, she made no connection between her bad temper and personal stress. 'As far as I'm concerned,' she said indignantly, her voice tight with emotion, 'the girls in the factory are to blame.'

But when Cindy really began to think about her state of mind, she admitted that events at home were affecting the situation at work. And when she was at work, she couldn't help dwelling on the problems at home. Her stress was fired by thoughts like:

Where on earth is Mike tonight? He said he would be home by eight. I'm sure he's not working. Things are falling to bits around here. He's never home on time and he never wants to go out with me anymore. I'm starting to look old; I'll soon be 40. I've wasted my life and I've got nothing to show for it.

With thoughts like this invading her mind, Cindy became more and more irritable at work. Then the obsessive thoughts began to escalate:

I'm losing my grip. These women are just slacking off. They need a rev up or we won't make quota and that'll be my fault. I'll be blamed, and if I'm laid off, I don't know how we'll make ends meet. Mike would be really pissed off and then he'd leave me for sure, and I'd be on my own with nothing ...

She recognised that emotionally she was reeling under the onslaught of either anxiety or anger. She also had marked physical symptoms of stress: headaches during the day, and at night she couldn't sleep.

Sometimes the effects of stress on your behaviour can be more subtle than this. Although your actions may have changed, on the surface these deviations don't appear to have anything at all to do with your thoughts or emotions. But if you understand the progressive stages of the stress cycle, you can see that any behavioural changes require the investigation of your thinking and your feelings.

> *Any behavioural changes require investigation of how you are thinking and feeling.*

There used to be nothing wrong with Jim's life. He was a talented dancer in his mid-twenties, good-looking and muscular and noted for his carefree manner. But one evening, during the performance of a difficult, very precise Balanchine piece, Jim momentarily lost concentration as he was turning a pirouette. He staggered and fell. Recovering quickly from his embarrassment, he danced out the remainder of his solo without a mistake and tried to put the fall out of his mind.

When the company began rehearsing a new program, Jim's confidence appeared to be intact, but once the performance season got under way, his self-assurance began to disintegrate. When Jim emerged on stage in front of a large audience, his body seemed to go haywire. His co-ordination was poor, his dancing out of time and sometimes he'd blank out completely and be unable to remember his steps. At first he was still dancing well in class, but as his public performances deteriorated, even his class work went downhill. He missed his cues, and his form, even in routine exercises at the barre, was sloppy. He said:

I used to be the best in the company and now I'm just a liability. I'm going to be kicked out if I can't get it together. I'm totally baffled and confused about why this is happening to me.

Jim cast his mind back to his fall in the Balanchine ballet. Recollecting how he had reacted to this, he was able to identify the kind of thoughts that had occurred the next time he had danced before an audience: 'What if I fall again? I must have looked like such an idiot. I've got to be really careful. If I make another mistake like that, I could injure myself. My career could be in danger.' As time went by, these thoughts expanded into a general criticism of his ability. 'My dancing's pathetic. I've lost my touch. I'm not in control of my body. I can't seem to relax anymore. My technique's shot to hell.'

After a few weeks, not only performances but also rehearsals and class work were accompanied by intense anxiety about whether he would dance well, and of course, he didn't. Describing himself as an emotional wreck, he spent sleepless nights worrying about the quality of the next performance. Jim's most obvious physical symptoms of stress were muscle tension and poor muscle co-ordination, which made it impossible for him to dance to his former standard. The effects of stress chemicals on his brain caused his mind to go blank and not remember his steps. He was trapped in a tailspin of negative cause and effect, until he was driven to confront the source of his fears.

Recognising burnout

Burnout is a form of depression that comes after prolonged effort and pressure. If this exertion pays off, or comes to an end early enough you may feel stress, but not the despondency and failure to cope which characterises burnout. Burnout occurs when it seems the job is unmanageable or never finished, no matter how hard you work. Your work feels like that of Sisyphus, the Greek mythological character who was condemned to Hades. His task was to endlessly push uphill a huge stone which, when he reached the top, always rolled down again.

> *Burnout occurs when it seems the job is unmanageable or never finished, no matter how hard you work.*

Burnout also robs you of your ability to relax. Nothing alleviates your conviction that you must be constantly on the alert, obsessing about the tasks and duties you have to perform, convinced that life can only be lived in a state of struggle. You can't read a magazine or watch television because you feel guilty that you're not working. You are tormented by the belief that there is not enough time for the thousands of onerous things you have to do. When you do occasionally permit yourself to go to a dinner party or meet a friend for coffee, you cannot concentrate on the conversation because you are exhausted and distracted. Gradually you begin to isolate yourself.

Rose was one of three partners who had recently formed a company which provided training programs for large corporations. The three women directors were dynamic and efficient with good track records in business. They had no difficulty attracting clients – in fact, the work poured in. But 18 months after the company was formed, Rose started to dread going to work. She said:

I feel there are too few of us making the decisions and I'm starting to question the validity of the decisions I make. I'm running on empty all day; I can't close the door on things at night. If I delegate something, it doesn't get done. Some of the people we have employed are absolutely incompetent and I feel I am becoming that way myself. I'm constantly frustrated and I feel burned out, because there's just too much to do. Even though I get up at five in the morning, I don't feel productive at all. I can't get through everything I set myself. The simplest things, like doing the dishes, turn into a major effort – I haven't done any laundry for two weeks.

Although Rose didn't realise that she was under stress, she did understand that changes had occurred in her ability to deal with her life. Immobilised by indecisiveness at work, her avoidance of useful activities at home, such as household tasks, contributed to a disordered atmosphere. In the mornings she delayed her departure for work as she went obsessively around the house, checking that doors and windows were locked and that household appliances were switched off. The time she devoted to this needless checking she might otherwise have spent more productively in doing the laundry or preparing a good breakfast. As she drove to work, she worried that she had left a door unlocked or a window open and she often returned home to check the security of the house one more time.

Eventually Rose detected the thoughts that were causing her stress. They ran like this:

The other two seem to be doing so well. What will happen if they find out I'm not coping? It's all too much, there's too much to do. Why did I get myself into this? I thought I could handle it, but I can't. There's just not enough support. My life is a nightmare. If I go on like this, I'll end up destroying the company.

Burnout, like all varieties of stress, reaches a terminal point where your body manifests the ineffectiveness of your mind, by refusing to function properly. Rose's stress manifested itself physically in effects on her brain and skin and muscles. Although she slept through the night, she woke feeling groggy and unrefreshed, her jaw aching with the effort of grinding her teeth all night. An itchy rash appeared on her chest and spread to her neck. As she had no known allergies, her doctor could do nothing but prescribe antihistamines, which quelled the rash but made her feel dehydrated and irritable. She couldn't think clearly and she had noticed that her memory was failing. Decisions were becoming beyond her and her work output was almost at a standstill. She stopped enjoying her work but even when she wasn't working she couldn't enjoy her free time. Finally, her doctor diagnosed her as depressed and prescribed her antidepressants.

Recognising the true cause of your stress

Many people arrive at a counsellor's office to discuss a problem that actually results from stress in other areas of their lives. A couple comes for counselling because their relationship is disintegrating, when the original reason for their differences may be that the husband has lost his job. A woman might make an appointment to discuss a discipline problem with her children, which, when she really looks at all the influences in her life, she sees is a result of her abrasive relationship with her own mother. Whenever she has an argument with her mother she yells at her children, who become upset and disobedient. Cindy's case, where her worries about her relationship were displaced into concerns about efficiency at work, is also an example of misidentified stress.

> *The source of your stress can often be misidentified.*

Numerous partnerships go to the wall during the year following the birth of a first child. Lack of sleep, worries about parenting and the strain on income if the mother has given up her job, all contribute to a stressful situation. As tempers fray, each partner looks negatively at his or her life. This negativity encourages a tendency to lay blame – usually on one's partner. He or she is too negligent, too fussy, too hysterical, too indifferent, and both of you are in a state of shock at the enormous changes the baby has wrought on your lives. In this atmosphere of recrimination, marriages begin to topple.

But these are not the only circumstances where the source of your stress can be misidentified.

Patricia was referred for therapy through her Employee Assistance Programme. She was young and bright and had never been intimidated by the man's world in which she moved as marketing manager of a large dairy company. Patricia had been with the company for two years, and for 20 months of that time she had been secure and relaxed in meetings and confident about the regular presentations she was required to make to the company. But over the last four months, her performance had plummeted. She said that now when she stood up to make a presentation:

My knees shake, my mind goes blank, I tremble. I dread the days that I have to give presentations. I think I just can't get up in front of all those people. I can hardly get out of bed, and twice I have called in sick.

She was baffled at the deterioration in her work and desperately keen to right it.

Discussions with Patricia revealed no obvious changes at work in the past four months that could have triggered this decline. But five months previously, Patricia had moved in with her boyfriend David, an MBA student. They had known one another for a year and although he could be possessive, Patricia was flattered by his intense interest in all her activities. Because of his studies, David had many opinions about business and commerce, which led to interesting conversations between them, and Patricia concluded that they were completely compatible. But after they set up house together it appeared to Patricia that David went through some sort of personality change. He became critical and controlling, especially about the way she did her job. He was constantly pointing out where Patricia deviated from marketing theory. He liked her to go over her presentations with him so he could critique them according to the information he was getting from his lectures. Also, since they had become a household unit, David expected her to function socially only as part of a couple. He disapproved of most of her friends and felt that if she went out without him, this constituted a slap in the face to their relationship. He also suggested to her that her appearance needed smartening up if she were to make a really effective impression at work.

I suppose I could see the warning signals there before, because he didn't like me going out on my own and we would often have arguments on the way home from parties where he'd accuse me of looking at somebody else all night. But after we moved in together, my life became like a prison. I got my hair cut because he thought it would look neater, but I hate it like this. We argue all the time, usually because something I've said or done irritates him. I still love him, and after we argue he is very good to me and he apologises and he says he knows he is difficult and it won't happen again, but over the course of a week or so it does. I feel that I have to watch everything I say now – he's so touchy. Nothing I do is right. I can feel my confidence just draining away, I feel constantly anxious. I lie awake at night trying to figure out what's gone wrong between us and I seem to have a headache all the time.

The actual source of Patricia's stress was David's emotionally abusive behaviour. She was carrying this stressful burden to work with her each day, where it severely affected her performance. When she thought closely about her problems at work, she saw many other changes in her behaviour. Not only had she become fearful during her presentations, she was also failing to plan her work commitments, which meant that she was no longer keeping up with deadlines or preparing properly for strategy meetings. Patricia realised that if she did not deal with the difficulties in her relationship, she would be heading for the dole queue.

Like many people who arrive for counselling, Patricia apologised for bothering the therapist with her trivial problems. 'I know it's stupid to complain about my boyfriend,' she said, 'when there are so many people with bigger problems. People with terminal illnesses and real tragedies in their lives.'

But stress is not trivial. It leaches through your life, advancing inexorably through its five stages, until you are actually a changed person, and changed for the worse. Your happiness and your health are under siege. Moreover, your state of mind affects others: your partner, your children, your colleagues. You owe it to yourself and those around you to take your distress seriously. You must realise that it is not the magnitude of an upsetting event that is the issue – that is, a car accident is not necessarily more devastating than verbal criticism – it is the effect that it has on you personally. What is a minor irritation to one person may be the death of the soul to another.

> *Once you identify that you are stressed, you can start to recognise what it is that stresses you and begin to liberate yourself from the problems that prevent you from maintaining control of your life.*

Summing Up

Recognise signals that you need to take control of your life:
- Is your thinking pessimistic?
- Are you in emotional turmoil?
- Does your body feel bad, is it breaking down?
- Are you behaving irrationally?

Get off the merry-go-round

The Five Step Life Plan

*Virtues are given to us neither by nature
nor against nature;
We are predisposed by nature to acquire them, but we
perfect them by practice.
We become fair by behaving righteously
And brave by behaving courageously.*

ARISTOTLE

Who controls your life?

I know but one freedom and that is the freedom of the mind.

ANTOINE DE SAINT-EXUPÉRY

You need to ask yourself who is in control of your life. If it's not you, it's
someone else – or it's destiny or fate. If it's destiny or fate, you have no personal
liberty. You're about as free as someone adrift in the Pacific in a rowboat without

oars. If you're not in control of your own life, you're certainly not free to do as you choose. Your greatest freedom lies in seeing the chains that bind you and knowing how to sever them.

> *Our biology and conditioning produce a vast amount of stress.*

We're all in bondage, first of all to our biology, and second to our conditioning. Together these operate to produce a vast amount of stress. You are free to the degree that you can understand fully the way your body operates and see the way people and events in your life have affected you in the past and in the present, and take action to change what is harmful to you.

Chapter 1 explained the way your biology takes control of you. Chapter 2 enlarged on the way the experiences of your life interact to make this worse. Both the beliefs and the values of your culture, and its agents – parents, teachers, friends and the other humans who influence you – may exert control over your life. Very little of your socialisation is planned and co-ordinated. Much of it is chance and will not necessarily produce the best possible outcome for you.

Researchers in neuro-science, the study of the way the brain operates, offer an interesting view on our ability to take charge of our lives. H. H. Kornhuber, an internationally renowned German neuro-scientist, has this to say:

> *The relationship between brain and mind is analogous to that between hardware and software in a computer. The software is not a function of the hardware: on the contrary, it makes the hardware work in a specific way. Whereas in species such as worms most of the software is an automatism of the network, in humans it is the result of education, culture, self-improvement and learning. It is everyday experience that to some extent we are able to change the programs operating in our brains at will. Brain software use that results in the formation of habits even influences the fine structure of the hardware (e.g. synapses).*

What Kornhuber is saying is that unlike lower organisms, humans are a species capable of changing their conditioning and to some extent even their biology.

Kornhuber also points out that while program development in the human brain is partly open to our own initiative, becoming more free is 'usually a laborious, gradual process of developing one's abilities, not a sudden jump to absolute freedom (as promised by some political ideologies and religious sects)'.

The implications of this are that you must understand the functioning of your body and your programming, and while you should not expect overnight miracles, or an effortless waltz through life, you must be persistent and resolute in changing programming that is harmful to you. If you keep wrestling with it, it will change; and once it is changed, it will stay that way unless you choose again to alter it.

> *You must be persistent and firm in changing programming that is harmful to you.*

What happens when you take successful action to overcome what is harmful to you? How does it change you as a person? What is the effect of overcoming your stress and taking control of your life? And how do you do this?

What happens when you take control?

You know subjectively that when you're not stressed, you feel calm and peaceful and more secure in yourself. You know too that if you've been confronted with a threatening situation and handled it well, you can feel elated and confident afterwards. These are the emotional feelings associated with a lack of stress or with overcoming stress. Do they have their counterpart in changes in your body's functioning?

You've probably accepted by now that one of the effects of stress on the body is its weakening of your immune system. You may have asked yourself if that destruction is permanent, or whether it can be repaired. If you damage your immune system, are you making yourself permanently vulnerable to illness? Do we have any scientific research on the effects, either on your immune system or your state of mind, of overcoming stress?

Albert Bandura and his associates at Stanford University have run a number of experiments investigating what happens to your immune system when you learn to control your stress. In one of these studies 20 people who were severely phobic about snakes learned to overcome their fear and to be able to tolerate a snake on their laps. This didn't happen all at once, of course. They were exposed to the snake over many sessions, each session increasing in its level of stress for them. They started by standing and watching the snake in its cage from across the room. When they felt comfortable with that, they moved on to the next step.

While they were being taught how to handle the snake, the researchers measured their heart rates and the amount of cortisol (a stress chemical) in their saliva; both of these are good indicators of stress levels. At the end of each session, the researchers took blood from them and measured their leucocyte, or white blood cell, levels so they could keep track of the effects on their immune systems. At the end of every session they also assessed each participant's level of self-efficacy, their belief in their ability to take charge of their life.

They discovered a number of interesting things. As the participants were trained to be able to handle the snake, their self-efficacy increased; they believed in themselves more. The most significant finding was that even though the physical symptoms of stress like pounding hearts and high levels of cortisol were present in all 20 people while they were being taught how to handle the snake, and their immune systems were impaired then, when they felt in control, that is, when their self-efficacy became high, their immune systems were not impaired – they were actually enhanced. More leucocytes were present in their blood than before the study started. These extra cells remained there over time.

> *Mastering your stress relatively rapidly raises your feelings of self-efficacy and can leave lasting protective changes in your immune system.*

Bandura concluded that mastering your stress relatively rapidly not only raises your feelings of self-efficacy but it can leave lasting changes in your immune system that may protect you against the effects of future stress. Those emotional feelings of elation and confidence that you get after you've risen to a challenge and carried it off well seem to have their physical counterpart in a stronger immune system. Their mental counterpart is found in a stronger belief in your ability to run your life well in the future. But this only happens if you get on top of your stress reasonably quickly. If stress lingers on and you have a hard time taking control of your life again, it has an opposite effect.

Other research evidence suggests that if control of your stress is gained more slowly and with difficulty you're likely to be left vulnerable to future problems. Chapter 2 explains in more detail why this may be. You can see that if it's been a long hard battle to get control of your stress, you may not be sure that you'll stay in control. You won't feel elated and confident afterwards; in fact, you may feel pessimistic and unsure and worry about whether you'll be able to handle the next onslaught. Negative thinking like this will get your stress reaction going again and the stress chemicals will continue to wear down your immune system.

Interestingly, even for animals controllability has been recognised as the key principle governing the effects of stress on the immune system. If animals are exposed to stress they are able to control, they also suffer no immune system damage. If they are unable to control their stressors, research has shown that their neuro-endocrine systems swing into action and their immune systems become damaged.

> *The message is clear: get on top of your stress fast*
> *and as effectively as you can.*

How do you stop the merry-go-round?

What is the most effective way to control your stress, to stop the merry-go-round and get off? The answer is that there is no one way; no single activity or technique or solution will keep you positive, happy and in charge of your life. Anyone who promises that is selling a lie. This is because stress is not just a single entity. It is composed of mental, emotional, physical and behavioural elements. Because you notice changes in your thinking, your feelings, your body and your behaviour when you're stressed, anything that proposes to control your stress must control or be able to change all four of these factors.

Are you a pessimist or an optimist?

> *We are all in the gutter, but some of us are looking at the stars.*
>
> OSCAR WILDE

Charles Carver and Michael Scheier are two American psychologists whose pioneering work in the area of optimism and stress management is relevant here. They make the point that for years people who stand outside the boundaries of psychology and science have said that being positive is good for you, but it's only recently that scientists have looked at whether this is truly the case, and if so, why. Now that the research has been done, it supports the belief that being positive about your life means you will be happier and healthier. Carver and Scheier have concluded that the reason for this is at least in part the way you handle your stress.

Those people who believe they will generally experience good outcomes rather than bad outcomes in their lives they labelled optimists. People who expect the worst outcomes they called pessimists. The two types of people not only feel differently about the world, they also behave differently. According to Carver and Scheier's work, if you're looking at the stars you will most probably pull yourself out of the gutter. They discovered that a major difference between optimists and pessimists lies in the way they handle stress and that this difference is why optimists are happier and physically healthier than pessimists.

> A *major difference between optimists and pessimists is in the way they handle stress.*

In Carver and Scheier's studies, the optimists dealt with their problems head on, taking active and constructive steps to sort out their situations. Optimists tackled their problems and solved them wherever they could. The pessimists were more likely to throw up their hands when the going got tough and give up on their goals. They were also more likely to ignore their difficulties, hoping they would go away. Optimists, on the other hand, accepted the reality of their situation rather than ignoring it. If they couldn't solve a problem, they tended to become philosophical about it and to change the way they looked at it. They did not act as emotionally or get as worked up about their difficulties as pessimists did. Optimists are active, but laid back about it. Pessimists are paralysed, but at the same time, worried sick. Optimists make changes in their thinking, in their emotions and in their behaviour; pessimists don't.

Scheier and Carver were interested in whether being an optimist was always the best way to be. They accepted that optimists would have the advantage in situations where problem-solving was possible, because they take constructive action more than pessimists do, but they wondered at first whether optimism might be detrimental in situations where action is not possible. Some situations cannot be changed: if you've had a death in the family, no constructive action will change that. If you've lost out on a job you wanted or crashed your car, these are misfortunes you cannot reverse. They look like uncontrollable situations.

The benefits of optimism

What the researchers found was that optimists had a whole host of what they termed 'emotion-focused' coping techniques for dealing with these sorts of problems. These included a willingness to accept that there was a problem, and an ability to put their situation in the best possible light and to grow personally from the difficulties they were facing. Optimists turned towards acceptance in uncontrollable situations, but pessimists turned towards denial. If you deny you have problems or refuse to accept that you're in trouble, you're trying to stick to a view of the world that isn't valid. By using denial to cope with stress, your life can accelerate even further out of control. If you're denying you have a problem, you won't even realise you may be able to do something to solve it, and your problem is likely to get worse as time goes by.

We've talked about the power of negative thinking. Given that pessimists certainly are negative thinkers, do we have any evidence about the bodily effects of pessimism? Martin Seligman and other researchers have found that having what they call 'a pessimistic explanatory style' is indeed harmful to you. What they mean by explanatory style is the explanation you give yourself for why events happen. This explanation affects what you expect the future to bring and it determines the extent to which you will feel helpless, out of control or depressed about bad events in your life. Some bad events are truly uncontrollable: 'My house burned down because it was struck by lightning'. But in many cases reality is ambiguous: 'My lover accepted a job in another city because it paid a lot more' or '…because she wanted to get out of our relationship'. Seligman believes that you have a characteristic way of explaining bad events where reality is ambiguous.

He says that if you have a pessimistic explanatory style, you will explain things as being stable: stable over time – 'It's going to last forever'; global – 'It's going to affect everything I do'; and internal – 'It's all my fault'.

In one of his studies, Seligman compared the immune systems of elderly people who were pessimistic about life with those who were optimistic. The pessimists had lower immune system levels than the optimists did. This was true regardless of any differences between the pessimists and the optimists in other factors which are known to affect immune levels: in their health, in their sleeping habits, in the amount of alcohol they drank and whether they were depressed or not.

> *Optimists are likely to have stronger immune systems.*
> *Their physical or emotional health problems are more likely*
> *to be temporary.*

This implies that an optimistic sick, sleepless, depressed, heavy drinker is likely to have a stronger immune system than a healthy, social-drinking pessimist. This sounds ridiculous, but it is not. Being an optimist means that any physical or emotional health problems are more likely to be temporary. Being a pessimist means that you are constantly stressed and wearing away your immune system. It looks like being negative will catch up with you in the end. And it may even affect your children. A ground-breaking study at the State University of New York at Stonybrook looked at the effects of maternal stress during pregnancy on whether babies had a low birth weight. These were mothers who were at risk of having their babies early because of medical problems. The results may surprise you. It was not the amount of stress mothers experienced while they were pregnant that caused their babies to be underweight but whether mothers were pessimistic or optimistic in general about their lives. The mothers who were least optimistic gave birth to the lowest weight babies.

However, you will see in Chapter 9 that latest research suggests it is not only that being an optimist allows you to manage stress better; positive thoughts also alter your biochemistry and make you more resistant to the effects of stress.

What do you do with your stress now?

Before you read on about how to free yourself from the chains of stress, have a good look at the way that you handle stress now. See if you know which of the four components of stress – mental, emotional, physical and behavioural – your methods of dealing with stress combat. Have you picked something that takes your mind off your problems? Or makes you feel better? Or are you using a technique to relax your body or change your behaviour? If you do this, you'll also be able to see whether it's just a partial solution and means that you need to add some more techniques. Very few techniques for handling stress address all four elements. This is true whether you have consciously figured out how to manage your stress, whether you have developed a way of handling it unwittingly in a kind of knee jerk reaction, or whether you use a technique that you have learnt at a stress management course or seminar.

> *Stress management techniques need to deal with the four components of stress: mental, emotional, physical and behavioural.*

Most methods of managing stress pick out only one of the four elements to deal with. Most people give up on their stress management techniques, or complain that they don't work when life really gets tough. But if you have selected a method of stress reduction that cannot reduce stress at all four levels, it can only be partially effective. Think about why this is. Remember the stress cycle and the way in which it is self-perpetuating? Your thoughts make you feel upset emotionally, which sets off the release of the chemicals and hormones that give you physical stress symptoms. One of these physical symptoms is the triggering of more negative thoughts, which make you feel more upset emotionally, and so the merry-go-round continues.

If your way of dealing with stress addresses only one of these four elements, the reduction you get will only be temporary because the cycle will keep going on its own. That doesn't mean that the method you've selected is ineffective, just that in itself it is not enough. But you're likely to assume that it isn't working at all, because your good feelings don't last and your stress starts to creep up again.

Addressing only one stress component

To make this clearer, let's look at some examples. If your most noticeable stress symptom is muscular tension and you choose massage to relax your tight muscles and stiff neck, you'll feel good for a while because you're going to get some decrease in your overall muscle tension and because, as recent research suggests, massage may release endorphins. You will hear more of these later in this chapter. But if, as soon as you get up from your massage, you start thinking about your problem, what do you think will happen? You're going to start feeling emotionally upset and because your thoughts will have set off the stress cycle, physical tension will inevitably follow.

You might say: 'But that's dealing with stress a long way down the line. A lot has happened before your muscles get tense.' What if you deal with the very beginning of the cycle: your thoughts? You might think that a method of stress reduction which helps you to think differently will be all you need, that if you banish negative thoughts you won't set off the stress cycle. This is the reason people select meditation, which is very effective during the 20 minutes or so that you spend doing it. But if you start dwelling once more upon your problems the moment the meditation ends, you will be back where you started.

Dealing with problem thoughts is an excellent way of dealing with stress, but it isn't enough on its own. If you look carefully at the habitual ways most people deal with stress, a lot of them do have the effect of changing your thoughts. If you come home from a hard day at the office and bury yourself in television to forget work, you're changing your thoughts. If you go and have a few drinks or pop a few pills to take your mind off your problems, you're doing exactly the same thing.

Alcohol

Having a few drinks is one of the commonest ways of dealing with stress; many people consider this socially acceptable. Unfortunately, alcohol may end up creating far more stress for you than it ever relieves in every area of your life. Alcohol puts a layer of fatty acids over negative thoughts as they move down from your cortex to your mid-brain where you feel emotions, so thoughts don't upset you as much. But alcohol also allows you to express emotions you later regret. If you feel emotional while you're drinking, you're far more likely to act on these emotions than when you're sober. This is because alcohol also puts a layer of fatty acids over the thoughts that would normally come down from your cortex and say, 'You feel like telling him what you think', or 'You feel like punching him out', or 'You feel like running off with his wife'. 'But don't do it!' You feel it, so you do it!

This characteristic of alcohol is called disinhibition and it is responsible for the apparent personality changes that come with drinking – the timid character who becomes the wolf at the office party, or the charmer who becomes nasty and abusive when drunk.

> *The more often you use alcohol to relieve your stress, the more likely you are to become dependent on it physically as well as psychologically.*

But alcohol not only causes changes in your behaviour, it can cause lasting changes in your life both physically and socially. We define an alcoholic now, not as the derelict in the gutter, but as someone for whom alcohol has produced problems in their relationships, their employment, their health, or with the law. The more often you use alcohol to relieve your stress, the more likely you are to become dependent on it physically as well as psychologically. Ten percent of people are alcoholic and there is without doubt a genetic predisposition to alcoholism. If someone in your family has an alcohol problem, you are at greater risk yourself of developing a problem if you choose alcohol to manage your stress. If drinking has made your partner or your children frightened of you or avoidant of you, if it has resulted in days off work because of hangovers, or jobs lost through incompetence, if it has resulted in brushes with the law through drink-driving, or violence towards others, or if it has caused you any one of the multitude of alcohol related disorders: heart problems, hypertension, gastro-intestinal ulcers, or cancers, chronic diarrhoea, and malabsorption, liver problems, sexual disfunctions, pancreatitis, pancreatic diabetes, anaemia, iron deficiency, brain damage, immune system problems, and many more – then alcohol is not only causing you stress, it is interfering with your ability to create a meaningful life.

Finding the right way to deal with stress

You can see that television is a relatively harmless form of stress management compared with alcohol and compared with drugs, which though a less common form of stress management than alcohol, also have the potential to create many of the problems alcohol does. However, all three of these in the end are inadequate because those problems that should be addressed are still there when you switch off the set or when you are no longer out of it.

> *You need to find a way of managing stress so that you deal with mental, emotional, physical and behavioural aspects at the same time.*

Even techniques like positive thinking about your situation or talking through your problems with a friend will be insufficient in themselves. Unfortunately, merely changing your attitude to a problem is not enough to prevent stress; some problems need action and simply looking at them in a more laid-back manner is not going to make them go away.

You may be the kind of person who swears by exercise to deal with stress, which is certainly part of an effective stress management plan. But like all other solutions, exercise alone is not enough. You will find that it will stop most of your physical symptoms of stress, but exercise doesn't prevent you from dwelling on your problems once you've stopped exercising, and thus starting the whole cycle off once more.

Is there a way of managing your stress so that you deal with all four aspects of it at once: mental, emotional, physical and behavioural, and at the same time enhance your life?

How to manage your stress and control your life: the Five Step Life Plan

What does it take to manage your stress and be in control of your life? There are five simple steps that will definitely achieve this. You may be able to eliminate your present stress entirely, or at least be able to deal effectively with major levels of stress and still live a well balanced and happy life.

But remember that this is an ongoing programme. You can't just do it for a month and forget about it, or you'll drift back to your old patterns. These five steps need to become part of the way you now look at the world. Why? Because stress cannot be eliminated from your life permanently and forever. That's unrealistic. You're never going to get rid of all your problems for good. New ones will crop up. The one thing you can be sure of in life is that it will deal you a lousy hand from time to time, but you need to be able to play that hand to your best advantage.

The Five Step Life Plan is discussed in more detail in later chapters, but here is a brief overview.

Fig. 6 The Five Step Life Plan

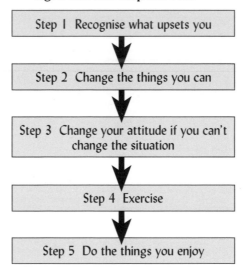

Step 1 Recognise what upsets you

Step 2 Change the things you can

Step 3 Change your attitude if you can't change the situation

Step 4 Exercise

Step 5 Do the things you enjoy

Step 1: Recognise what upsets you

If you want to be in control of your stress, you need to be very clear about exactly what it is that stresses you. If you can attack your problems before they set off the stress cycle, you save yourself emotional anguish, physical trauma and further stress. If you don't know what the causes of your problems are, then you can't decide what to do about them.

Recognising your stress as soon as possible means knowing what you're saying to yourself about your problems. The thoughts in your head trigger everything else that follows. If you don't think negative thoughts, you don't feel negative feelings and you don't get negative physical symptoms. However, you need to be alert not only to your thoughts, but to your individual physical and emotional symptoms of stress. As you saw in Chapter 3, it is common to suffer from stress and be unaware of it. Knowing where your body shows its stress gives you extra insurance against stress. It alerts you to the fact that your life is getting out of control and allows you to take hold of it again before it slips into chaos.

Ways of recognising what upsets you and the way it affects you are detailed in Chapter 5.

Step 2: Change the things you can

You can get rid of many problems in your life by taking some positive action, since action is what distinguishes optimists from pessimists. You may be the kind of person who prefers to stick your head in the sand and avoid difficulties, but that's not going to get you anywhere. If you front up to problems, analyse them carefully, either on your own or with someone else, you'll be surprised at what you can solve. Positive actions can change all four components of stress. Solve your problem so that it's no longer a concern, then you won't be prey to the upsetting thoughts that start the stress cycle.

Ways you can change what you need to, and the skills that will help you to do this, are covered in Chapter 6. There are some things, though, that you can't change, which brings us to the next step.

Step 3: Change your attitude if you can't change the situation

Often the causes of your most severe pain cannot be changed. The bitterest regrets and the most tormenting guilt are usually about the past. If you let them stay with you they can shatter your happiness for today and for years to come.

Truly, the past can poison the present, but it is not only regrets about yesterday that are destructive: fears about tomorrow can be too. Objectively, you probably realise that most of what you dread happening never eventuates, but you can still make your life a nightmare by worrying that it might. Many people spend their lives regretting the past and fearing the future and never really living for today at all.

To combat this, you need a way of changing your own attitude to problems, because if you can't change a situation, the thing that you can change is your attitude to it. To control your life, you need a mechanism for switching off thoughts that trouble you about situations you cannot change, and you need a way of looking at these situations more positively.

Changing your attitude also changes all four components of stress: mental, emotional, physical and behavioural. If you don't think the thoughts that distress you, you won't activate the cycle.

Ways you can switch off thoughts that upset you, change your own attitudes, and think positively are covered in Chapter 7.

Step 4: Exercise

Aerobic exercise is absolutely essential to any adequate stress management and life enhancement program because it is the only thing that gets rid of the stress hormones and chemicals that have been pumped into your bloodstream. If you don't exercise, they accumulate; they don't dissipate. Your liver may metabolise some of them but not enough. Aerobic exercise increases your heart rate and drives your blood out of the central core of your body where it accumulates in stress, and into your large muscles. These muscles use up as energy all the chemicals in your blood that have been circulating in the central core of your body, affecting all your organs and giving you the physical symptoms of stress, and producing more negative thinking.

> *Exercise deals with the physical effects of stress,*
> *and to some extent with the mental effects.*

Once you exercise, all your physical symptoms of stress stop, because the stress chemicals no longer speed up your internal organs, and it stops your negative thinking. Provided you don't go on thinking negatively, which you won't if you have been following Steps 2 and 3, your head will be clearer and you'll feel calm and more optimistic after you've finished. In fact, positive thoughts are increased because exercise releases from your brain other chemicals of a different nature to the stress chemicals. The amino acids known as endorphins are painkillers and mood elevators. They make you feel positive and confident, helping to counter the negativity of your thinking caused by the depressant activity of the stress hormones and chemicals. Exercise deals with the physical effects of stress, and also to some extent with the mental effects, through the endorphins it releases.

Chapter 8 covers most of the information you need to design an effective exercise program and to stick to it.

Step 5: Do the things you enjoy

While it is clear that doing things you enjoy is related intimately to living a fulfilling life, what is the relationship between enjoyment and stress management? One of the first things you learn in psychology textbooks is that perception is unitary. You can only think about one thing at a time. If you're concentrating on things that you enjoy, you're not going to be dwelling on things that upset you. Doing things that you enjoy stops the stress cycle before it gets started. It acts, in part, to prevent stress in your life.

Doing things that you enjoy takes your mind off what upsets you, but also increases your sense of mastery and control.

But doing things that you enjoy has a far greater effect than merely taking your mind off your stress for a brief period. Enjoyments and achievements increase your sense of mastery and control over your world, supplying a sense of balance to your life so that it doesn't ever seem hopeless. They allow you to reassure yourself that although one part of your life is going wrong, at least not all of it is bad news.

Doing things you enjoy has another interesting effect. Some enjoyable activities release endorphins into your system or affect your mood chemically in other ways. Knowing which activities these are allows you to plan a life that will keep you positive, happy and feeling good. And as mentioned earlier in this chapter, there is even evidence now that merely thinking positively alters your biochemistry in some way that decreases your stress.

Chapter 9 helps you decide whether your life is balanced or not, to identify the things you enjoy, those that release endorphins, as well as those that do not, and to plan the life you want to live.

Now you are ready to start your Five Step Life Plan. From now on you are going to take control, not your body, nor your conditioning, not other people and not fate.

Summing Up

♦ Taking control of your life boosts your confidence and your
  immune system.
♦ You will be happier and physically healthier if you are an
  optimist, not a pessimist.
♦ Analyse the way you deal with your stress now.
♦ Find out about the Five Step Life Plan and why it will work
  for you.

  Step 1:   Recognise what upsets you.

  Step 2:   Change the things you can.

  Step 3:   Change your attitude if you can't change
              the situation.

  Step 4:   Exercise.

  Step 5:   Do the things you enjoy.

Getting started

Step 1: Recognise what upsets you

All our knowledge is ourselves to know.
ALEXANDER POPE

Getting in touch with your thoughts and feelings

To manage your stress properly and be entirely in control of your life, it is vital to be closely in touch with your thoughts and your feelings – both your emotional and physical feelings.

> *If you are very clear about what upsets you and about the effects of every stage of the stress cycle, you will be in a better position to recognise you're stressed and to do something about it.*

The best way to identify what is stressing you is to recognise the causes as they happen. Remember that stress can be considered an umbrella term for any negative emotion so it's not just things that cause you anxiety you're recording here. It is important to keep a running record of exactly what stresses you for a week or two before you develop your Life Plan. When you ultimately come to put your stress management techniques to work, you will be doing this on the spot, as soon as you start thinking negatively, therefore you need to be able to recognise these negative thoughts as soon as you start thinking them. The best way for you to keep a running record of your stress is to keep a stress diary.

The value of a diary

If you keep a diary of the things that upset or stress you, you will learn a lot about yourself. You may think that you know your personality, but much of what you record in your diary will surprise you. To begin with, you will get a very clear idea of exactly what is not right in your life. You'll learn which events cause you most stress – they're often not the ones you expect. You will be able to see exactly what you're saying to yourself about them and to understand how they affect you emotionally. Remember, the content of your thoughts determines what your emotions will be. By paying close attention to your physical symptoms at the time you're feeling these emotions, you will become very aware of just how your thoughts and emotions affect you physically. You're likely to discover some surprising symptoms.

> *Keeping a diary lets you know when and what upsets you, and how it affects you physically. It also sets a benchmark from which you can see changes.*

Once you have experienced the effects of your thoughts and emotions on your body, you'll have a good understanding of your physical weaknesses. You'll know which part of your body is likely to break down if you don't deal with your stress. For example, if your stomach churns every time something stressful happens, it's a fair assumption that you're probably ulcer material if you let things build up for too long. If your heart is always going flat out when you get upset, watch out for heart attacks in your later years.

By keeping a running record of the things that upset you, you'll also find out a lot of other fascinating information. You may find that little things you thought were reasonably trivial appear again and again in your diary – this means they are much more significant than you thought and need to be dealt with. You will come to understand the pattern of your stress, too. You will find out when you get upset most easily: at work, at home, socially.

These records provide a baseline for you, a benchmark from which you can see the changes you're making. If you find that you've been upset 30 times in the week prior to starting your plan, that is, in the first week you kept your diary, and only three times in the fourth week once you're well into it (and this kind of decrease is very common), then you know you're getting somewhere, that what you are doing is working.

When you take notes on your own behaviour, you often look at what you're recording and you say to yourself, 'Why on earth am I getting stressed over that? It's such a trivial thing to worry about!' You find that you spontaneously change your attitude to some of the things that upset you.

Whether this happens or not depends on how you interpret your notes: If you think, 'Well I'm getting stressed about too many trivial things', then you will become more laid back. But if you think, 'There are a lot more things wrong in my life than I thought before I started', you'll probably get even more stressed.

Keeping your stress diary

What do you record? How do you record it? And how do you analyse it at the end of a week? You will write in your stress diary the thought that upsets you, and which starts off the whole stress cycle, the emotion it causes you, and the physical changes that you feel in your body afterwards.

You may not be able to recognise all your stressful thoughts at the beginning of your first week of recording. Don't worry if you can't identify what you're actually saying to yourself. Simply write down the event or the situation that made you feel upset. When you look back on this, you'll probably find that you can work out the thought that caused you stress.

Write down how you feel about it. The emotions you feel may be mixed. It's perfectly possible to feel a combination of feelings about a specific incident. A relationship that has come to an end may leave you feeling both angry and regretful. Asking the boss for a raise may cause you both anxiety and embarrassment.

Try to identify what changes you feel in your body while you're thinking about the problem. These are your physical symptoms of stress. Turn back to Chapter 1 to the checklist of all the physical effects of stress on the body. Identify which of these you feel when you are upset about something or when you know you are stressed. Recognise them as your warning signs. If you feel them, even if you don't think your life is getting out of control, start looking! They could be the first tremors that set off the avalanche.

These symptoms are danger signals. When you feel them, take them as a tip-off that you're already well down the road to losing control. If you're waking in the middle of the night or constantly fighting off headaches or migraines, or sighing a lot, watch out. Things in your life are not the way you'd like them to be.

> *Your stress diary records the thought that upsets you, and which starts off the whole stress cycle, the emotion it causes you, and the physical changes that you feel in your body afterwards.*

How to take your notes
To begin your stress diary start a fresh page in your notebook and rule it up into a date column and four main columns, with the following headings:

- Date
- What Happened
- What I Thought
- What I Felt Emotionally
- What I Felt Physically

Take notes on thoughts that upset you. Where you can't identify your thoughts, record the events that upset you. Don't write a lot, just a word or a line. Write down how you felt emotionally about each of these and how your body felt at the same time. Write everything down as it happens.

It isn't necessary to write down screeds of information. You can write a word or a phrase, as long as it's sufficient to recall at the end of the week exactly what it was that made you record it. It is critical to make these notes as the stress occurs. If you try to write them at the end of the day, you will have forgotten half of what stressed you. This is because some of the things that upset you will be very fleeting: brief thoughts that flit in and out of your mind. Nonetheless, when you come to manage your stress, they need to be dealt with on the spot, otherwise they set off the stress reaction. If they are not dealt with, they will continue to build up. Keep your diary on you, and a pen to record things as they happen.

Remember that it is important to record this information for at least a week before you try any of the techniques listed in later chapters to manage your stress. When you've done this for a week or two, you'll become expert at identifying what stresses you and how it affects you. Then you are in a strong position to work out the best way to approach your troubles.

Analysing your stress diary

1. Once you have a week or two of records, sit down with your stress diary and check out the physical feelings you experience when you're stressed and the emotions that accompany your stress. Make a list of them. Know that they are your warning signals. When they happen, you're thinking about something that upsets you. Your thoughts are becoming negative and you're on the merry-go-round.

2. Now analyse the specific causes of your stress. What makes you feel upset? Is there a pattern? Does it happen only at work, or does it happen at home and in social situations as well? Do you have many sources of stress or only one or two? Look at the problems that recur frequently. These are likely to be the most serious.

3. On another page of your stress diary make a separate list. If you've repeatedly made a note about someone you work with or about your boss, then write down 'difficult relationship with workmate' or 'difficult relationship with boss'. If you find that you're constantly thinking about something that happened in the past – for example, you bought a house last year and you feel that you paid too much for it – write that down as one topic as well. If you're dwelling on some real or imagined inadequacy about yourself, add that to your list.

Now you are ready to start dealing with these problems by designing your own Life Plan. Read the next two chapters. By the time you have finished them, you will have decided which of your problems you can take action on, and which of them you cannot change but must look at differently.

> *Your Life Plan: Step 1*
> 1. *Keep a diary for at least a week of the things that upset you.*
> 2. *Note your thoughts, emotions and physical symptoms of stress.*
> 3. *Record everything as it happens.*
> 4. *Analyse your diary: list your thoughts, emotions and physical feelings and the problems that cause these.*

We now pick up again the story of Paul the businessman dreading his trip to Boston, and the stress management plan he designed for himself. You will see from Paul's vacillations that real life is not always as straightforward as the textbooks would have it. You too may find it takes you a while to get nice neat tidy records – but persevere, it gets easier when you get to Step 5.

Paul's Life Plan: Step 1

I bought a small black notebook that was to be my stress diary. I carried it around with me for several days without opening it. For some reason I felt self-conscious about writing in it and I told myself I was too busy to spend time recording every little thing that was happening. There were always a thousand other things that seemed more important – telephone calls, meetings, lunch, a TV program I thought I should watch – but all the time my eye was on the calendar, knowing that I would have to go to Boston and present myself as a credible person. My feelings of dread about it refused to go away.

And then I had a really bad 24 hours. I felt like a man trying to plug a dyke with his little finger while a major flood of causes and effects was cascading over me. I felt like I was about to be swept away into chaos and I'd end up professionally dead. These were the main events: It was my wife Becky's birthday. I'd bought her some perfume, but the birthday breakfast didn't go well. I was jumpy and bad-tempered for no good reason. I said that I would drop the kids off at school on my way to work, but I couldn't seem to get myself organised to leave the house, so Becky ended up doing it. She gave me a look as if to say, 'Can't I ever rely on you?' I was thinking about the fax I'd have to send when I got to work. It was just straightforward information that needed sending to Head Office, but I'd got it into my head that I had made a mistake with the projections and thought I'd have to delay sending the fax so I could check the figures again.

I arrived at work late, which put me on the back foot right away. I was useless at work. Then the tailspin started. The manager from Boston called through, wanting to know why I hadn't faxed the figures. While he was talking to me I went completely blank. I realised I hadn't listened to a word he had said. I think he'd asked me a question, but I had no idea how to reply. I completely lost it. All I could think about was getting out of the office. So I started to say something – I don't remember what – some bland statement and then I put down the phone in the middle of talking so that he would think we had been cut off. I felt an utter fool. I rushed past my secretary, muttering something about being called to an urgent meeting. She looked at me like I was crazy. Then I got in the car and drove home.

I couldn't cope with the motorway, so I drove through the suburbs. I hardly knew where I was driving. I was dimly aware that Becky and I were supposed to be going out that night for dinner, but I couldn't remember which restaurant or what time and this made me feel even more panicky and out of control. Then to top everything off, when I swung into the driveway I clipped our stone wall and smashed a headlight. Somehow I got through the evening, got through the dinner. We'd taken a cab so I didn't have to drive and so I drank a huge amount of wine, which is unlike me. I went to sleep in a stupor but woke around 3 a.m. and couldn't get back to sleep. In the morning I couldn't face the prospect of going into the office, so I asked Becky to call and say I had food poisoning, although I was sure that everyone at work would know that was a lie.

I lay in bed all morning. I didn't want to talk to anyone. I was pleased that Becky had to go out. Finally I got up, had a shower and forced myself to have some coffee and toast. I thought, if I don't get to grips with this thing, I really am going to lose my job. I felt desperate. So I grabbed a piece of paper and wrote at the top of it:

What Is Wrong Now?
- *I'm going to blow this trip to Boston. I'm not preparing properly for it and when I get there and they see how incompetent I am, they'll blame me for the company's bad performance. My boss is in Boston right now wondering what the hell is happening. How can I explain why I'm not at work?*
- *I ruined Becky's birthday.*

- *There are problems in our relationship.*
- *I'm out of touch with the kids.*
- *I'll have to get the car and the fence repaired.*
- *We spent too much money on the bathroom renovations.*
- *I've got this weekly commitment to play squash with Don, but I'm always cancelling. He's getting pissed off with me.*
- *I think there might be something seriously wrong with Dad. He had a skin graft on his hand last month, but he won't talk to me about it.*
- *I don't like my wife taking Spanish lessons.*

What Do I Think?

I spent two hours in the kitchen writing all these things down, thinking hard about my life. It was quite an emotional experience. I thought I must be some kind of terrible pessimist because I just love to see the bad side of everything. I mean I was getting pretty disconnected from reality. When I really thought about it, I realised that when I was getting ready for work in the morning, standing at the bathroom mirror, shaving, running through in my mind the things that I would have to do that day, a little voice in my head was always saying, 'You're a failure Paul. You know that meeting's going to be a hassle. You're going to have a lot of explaining to do'. And yet if I really was a failure, how come I have this job and a decent CV and a family and a nice house? I was so sick of living in this permanent black fog.

What Do I Feel About It Emotionally?

Despairing, helpless and despising myself constantly.

Where Do I Feel It Physically?

I feel sick. I'm always feeling sick. I wake up every morning with diarrhoea. Just thinking about these things makes my stomach lurch and my heart beats faster. I'm looking at my left hand now while I'm writing and it's clenched in a fist. I feel like I want to burst into tears, and to stop that happening I have to breathe faster, and this act of control also means that my muscles feel tighter. I realise now that these sensations happen to me several times a day, and I guess that's why, when I fall into bed at night, my whole body is aching.

Okay, I thought, I'll commit myself to the stress diary. How could it make me feel any worse?

My Stress Diary

After a week I had several pages I could look back on. Some of it looked like this:

Date: Monday 5th

1. *What happened: Becky silent at breakfast.*
2. *What I thought: She's really fed up with me.*
3. *What I felt emotionally: Panic. She'll leave me.*
4. *What I felt physically: Sick in the stomach. Heart pounding.*

1. *Received astronomical consultant project manager's invoice.*
2. *He thinks he can take me for a ride on this.*
3. *Anxiety about escalating costs: I should have intervened.*
4. *Sweating. Headache. Heart pounding.*

1. *Went to buy late lunch at Victoria Café, but they'd just closed the kitchen.*
2. *You could make an exception for me. I'm a regular and you could at least make a sandwich for me to take away. I don't have time to go somewhere else for food.*
3. *Frustration and anger.*
4. *Headache worse.*

1. *Lost to Don at squash. He smirked and told me I'm not fit.*
2. *I hate squash and I hate losing. Don thinks I'm useless.*
3. *Anger and inadequacy.*
4. *Exhausted.*

1. *Kids playing game on my computer.*
2. *They could accidentally get into one of my files and destroy my work.*
3. *Anger. They're spoilt brats who won't listen to me.*
4. *Headache. Sweating. Heart pounding.*

1. *Becky gone to Spanish class without saying goodbye.*
2. *You don't care about me. You're blaming me for something.*
3. *Jealousy and anxiety. Depression.*
4. *Shaky. Tearful.*

Analysing my Stress Diary

When I read back on a fortnight of entries, I was surprised to see patterns emerging. I thought that the office was the place where I was most stressed. But although I had entries for many things that occurred at work, I was alarmed to see that I had just as many entries around my relationship with Becky. And more than once, I had written down the emotion 'jealousy' connected with Becky. I was really taken aback to see this. I wondered if my dread at going to Boston had something to do with the fact that I would be away from home rather than what would actually happen in Boston. Also, I saw that under the heading 'What I felt' was a recurring sense of inadequacy: like I wasn't important; that people wouldn't really pay attention to me. There were a lot of entries about my squash games with Don, which seemed out of proportion, because Don isn't all that important to me. I was stunned that I regarded the world as such a hostile place – like nothing was going to happen without a battle. If I looked out of the bedroom window and saw junk mail blowing around the lawn, it drove me crazy. I'd think, how dare someone litter my lawn! I'd think about how I was going to track down the direct mail companies and deliver loads of junk mail back to them, so they would know what it felt like to have this unsolicited garbage dumped on them. When I read these reactions of mine, I was struck by how exhausting it was to let something this trivial occupy my thoughts. I was spending a great deal of time getting hung up on nothing. I thought, boy, you're really programmed to turn anything into a problem.

I started to re-examine some of the entries. For instance, when I was furious because the kids had used my computer though I had asked them not to. I was thinking, well Paul, you've got a very fixed way of seeing things, because you think that the event is about the kids disobeying you. In your head that means they don't respect you, that they think so little of you as a father, they'll sabotage something important to you. Come on. That's extreme. What about: They just felt like playing Kidpix and forgot that they weren't supposed to? It's not that personal. It's not even that important. I started to think about what was important to me. I was expecting the word 'Boston' to leap into my head like it always does. But the word I saw in my mind's eye was 'Becky'.

Summing Up

Start your Life Plan:

Step 1: Recognise what is wrong in your life now

- Find out about yourself: keep a diary.
- Get in touch with your thoughts and feelings.
- Analyse what you will change in your life.

Take action

Step 2: Change the things you can

The bitterest tears shed over graves
Are for words left unsaid and deeds left undone.

HARRIET BEECHER STOWE

Why confront your problems?

Where you can take some action to change what stresses you, take that action. Don't pull a paper bag over your head and hope that your problems will solve themselves; they won't, they'll get worse. That kind of gloomy passivity is the mark of a pessimist. It's guaranteed to cause unhappiness and illness and thwart all your desires.

Even if the action you need to take is really tough, like changing something about yourself, take it! If you don't, your stress will magnify itself. You'll see the whole world as an antagonistic place and you'll create more problems for yourself. Like a creeping cancer, your stress once started, grows, destroying more and more of your health and happiness.

> *Where you can take some action to change what stresses you,*
> *take that action. If you are dissatisfied with something*
> *in your life, change it.*

If you are dissatisfied with something in your life, change it. By doing this you will increase your self-efficacy. Chapter 4 discussed the effects on your immune system of taking action to overcome your fears. Bandura's research on self-efficacy also shows that the more control you exert over the events in your life, the more you come to believe you can change your life. Taking charge has a spin-off effect – it's like the vicious cycle of stress, but in reverse. Once you start believing in yourself, the research shows you will continue to take charge of your life. You will continue to alter your circumstances if they're not the way you want them to be, and you will reach more of your goals.

On the other hand, the research on learned helplessness shows that you make more stress for yourself if you don't change the things in your life that you can change. If you always fail to take control of events, or if you're unable to, you become both depressed and powerless, and unmotivated to take charge of your life.

Taking action to confront and change your situation when you're almost paralysed with fear can help you to break the control of the fear. Action is the antidote to despair. People who are severely agoraphobic cannot move outside their houses without suffering crippling attacks of panic. Studies have shown that if you encourage them first to walk outside their door, then to walk a few steps down the path, then to walk out to the gate, and gradually increase the distance from the security of their home, you can teach them to overcome their phobia. They learn that they can deal with the panic symptoms, and in the end they disappear. At this point they no longer have to remain prisoners in their own homes.

It's the same principle that Albert Bandura used in his work with people who were phobic about snakes: take action, make the changes gradual, stick at them. Taking action to address the cause of your stress has also been shown to be beneficial with many other fears and phobias too.

The evidence is compelling: if you don't tackle your troubles, they'll destroy you; if you do tackle them, you'll become stronger.

Even in situations where you could be said to be justified in feeling powerless, being able to change some aspect of your circumstances will make you happier and less stressed and more likely to confront your problems in the future.

Decide which problems in your stress diary you can change

Once you've completed a list of separate problems in your life, then take a good look at it and ask yourself, 'Which of these can I take some constructive action on, and which of them can I not change?' Leave aside for a moment the ones that you cannot change. We'll deal with them in Chapter 7. They are causes of stress that you can't change by action, but you can change by altering your attitude to them.

You may be asking now, 'How can I tell the difference between situations that I should look at differently and those I should actively take charge of and change?' Say to yourself, 'What can I possibly do about this? Is there anything at all that will make this situation different?' In most cases it will be obvious whether there is some action you can take. If you're still not quite sure how to tell those you can change from those you can't, take a quick look at page 146 in Chapter 7, which outlines the kinds of problems that can't be changed.

How to change what you can

1. Make a list of the problems for which you can take some constructive action.
2. Ask yourself what specifically needs changing about them so that they will no longer upset you, and write down these solutions.
3. Now make a plan for when and how you'll carry them out.
4. Next, decide when and how you're going to evaluate the solutions you've chosen, so that you can check out whether they're working. Evaluation is important because most plans need to be adjusted from time to time. Circumstances, and sometimes your own priorities and values, may change. Also you can never entirely predict how you are going to feel about something before it happens.

Try the solutions to your problem for two or three months, which is usually long enough to see whether something is going to work. If your stress hasn't gone by then, go back to the drawing board. Either try something else or look at the next section on troubleshooting.

> *If your attempts at changes don't work, look at the troubleshooting section.*

Troubleshooting

It sounds easy to take charge of your life in this way and to make these changes, and it is, but it may not always be entirely straightforward. What should you do if you know you can change what is stressing you but you're not sure what is the best way to do this? You may want to try some of the things discussed below. The first is to seek advice.

> *Troubleshooting may involve:*
> ♦ *Getting advice for practical and emotional problems.*
> ♦ *Other therapies, such as Thought Field Therapy.*
> ♦ *Problem-solving techniques.*

Advice for practical problems

Who should you ask for advice? This really depends on whether your problem is practical or emotional. If it is the former, and it has something to do with finance, talk to your bank manager or an accountant or to a budget adviser or a financial planner, whichever is appropriate. If it's your health that's giving you stress, talk it out with your doctor, or seek out a specialist if you're not satisfied with what your doctor has said. If you're stressed about work, decide who is the appropriate person to consult and seek their advice.

Sometimes you'll find that you only need to sit down with a friend, someone whose viewpoint you trust and whom you know has no axe to grind. In doing this you can get an objective, unbiased view of your problem and can then work out the action you must take.

How to find the right advice for emotional problems

If your problem is about a relationship, talk it through with a therapist. Don't let yourself feel inadequate because you are seeking professional advice on personal matters. Look at it this way: if you're not an expert in a field, it makes good sense to find someone who is. You don't try to fix your car or your washing machine if you know nothing about mechanical matters; you're relieved to put your possessions in the hands of someone who is an experienced tradesperson. So why feel bad about putting your relationship in the hands of someone who has spent a number of years studying and fixing relationships and personal problems?

> *If your problem is about a relationship, or you need to learn relationship skills, consult a therapist.*

There are fewer barriers today against seeking help for problems that are emotional than there used to be. People are more aware of the value to be gained from properly qualified and trained psychological therapists. Most people realise that they get far less instruction or training in how to keep themselves mentally healthy than they do in ways of maintaining physical health.

It is not only advice on relationships that you may need assistance with. Sometimes you need to learn a particular skill that will enhance your relationships, like positive parenting.

My parents were only 18 when I was born – they got married because Mum was pregnant and I think they resented me because I was the reason. They were pretty tough on me when I was a kid; my earliest memories are ones of fear. We get on okay now, I understand what they must have gone through and I've forgiven them, I guess. I thought I'd put it all behind me, but I'll tell you what devastated me: when my son was born, I found myself doing exactly what they did to me – shouting and swearing and getting angry with him. I went looking for help right away.

Or, you may want to learn from a professional one of the new so-called Energy Psychology therapies; these are beyond the scope of this book to teach you.

Thought Field Therapy

Recently, several therapies have emerged that reportedly produce rapid therapeutic results, often within a matter of minutes. An interesting new book, part of the Innovations in Psychology series, discusses research which compared four therapeutic techniques capable of causing lasting and profound emotional changes in a single session: Visual Kinaesthetic Dissociation; Eye Movement Desensitisation and Reprocessing; Traumatic Incident Reduction; and Thought Field Therapy. The author of the book, Fred Gallo, describes these as causing changes in the body's energy fields. Of the four techniques, the one that worked fastest was Thought Field Therapy. Thought Field Therapy is also the only one of the four you can easily learn to apply yourself.

When you hear it described, Thought Field Therapy may sound to you like magic – or hocus pocus. But it has been shown capable of eliminating the uncontrollable emotions of post-traumatic stress disorder in a one-hour session. The developers of Thought Field Therapy and its variants (Roger Callahan and his students, Gary Craig, Larry Nims and others) claim it can remove or neutralise any unwanted emotion, positive or negative. You may ask why you would want to get rid of a positive emotion, but think about the decrease in your stress level if you could change the overwhelming desire to drink or gamble, or the pain of unrequited love. Therapists have taught people to use Thought Field Therapy to remove the emotional and behavioural effects of past traumas, anxieties, phobias, panic attacks and addictions. Using it, you can even learn to control obsessive compulsive disorder, pain and depression.

How Thought Field Therapy works

Various explanations have been given as to how Thought Field Therapy works. But as yet there is no sound neuro-scientific research on how it alters brain functioning, although practitioners will tell you there is no doubt that it does this. Thought Field Therapy is based on tapping specific acupuncture or acupressure points on the upper body while, at the same time, thinking about the aspect of yourself you wish to become unemotional about. For example: the individual traumatic memories of your childhood, your anxiety about tomorrow's job interview, your feelings about the lover who has left you.

*Thought Field Therapy is based on tapping specific acupuncture
or acupressure points on the upper body while, at the same time,
thinking about the aspect of yourself you wish to
become unemotional about.*

One explanation of the way Though Field Therapy may work, easier to understand than the alterations in energy fields presented by Callaghan and others, is based on what is now known about acupuncture. Although in the past acupuncture has been surrounded in mystery and scepticism, you know by now that the way the brain and the body communicate is through the release of chemicals. All energy fields, forces, or 'healing power within' can be expressed via secretion of these chemicals. Ancient systems of healing that use terminology we now consider non-scientific may be stating in different terms the same principles of signalling between brain, mind and body, and body and mind that scientists are now working out at the cellular and molecular level.

Acupuncture

Acupuncture is now generally accepted as orthodox medicine. Medical schools run courses in acupuncture for doctors, physiotherapists use it routinely, and we know something about how it works. Acupuncture does two things. First, it releases into your bloodstream chemicals known as endogenous opioids; among these are enkephalins and endorphins. Both these chemicals are painkillers, and since acupuncture is usually prescribed for pain, endogenous opioids explain part of acupuncture's effectiveness. However, endorphins are also 'uppers' (or mood elevators), so if you think about something that causes you emotional pain, or an unwanted emotion, while your body is in a state of endorphin arousal, as you do in Thought Field Therapy, it appears to neutralise the effect of that emotion.

Second, acupuncture alters the ability of the nerve pathways to transmit pain messages. In the same way, it appears that thinking about something that causes you an unwanted emotion, while you are actively releasing endorphins into your bloodstream, alters the responsiveness of the pathways which run from the cortex of your brain into the mid-brain, or limbic system, where you feel your emotions, and down to the adrenal and pituitary glands that produce the chemical reactions of the stress cycle. By the end of your Thought Field sequence, you can think about your problem, but you experience no emotion and no behavioural follow on.

Acupuncture releases chemicals that are natural painkillers and also alters the ability of the nerve pathways to transmit pain messages.

The enormous significance of removing unwanted and negative emotions is not only that you will reduce your stress and feel happier, but that you will not carry out the kind of behaviour that so often follows overwhelming anxiety, phobias, addictions and obsessions. You can also use Thought Field Therapy to rapidly eliminate the intense emotions which are attached to traumatic memories of your past and which make you more vulnerable to stress.

Problem-solving

If you're not sure about the best way to change your situation, and you decide that you don't want to seek professional advice or discuss your troubles with someone else, try a technique called problem-solving. This will enable you to look clearly at all the possible options for solving your problems, to evaluate the pros and cons of each, and to select the one which will work best.

Problem-solving techniques provide you with a structured way of finding solutions for the things that trouble you.

Fig. 7 (overleaf) outlines the steps that you need to take:

Step 1: Define your problem

Frequently, if you can't sort out what needs to be changed in your life, it is because you haven't clearly and concisely defined what the problem is. Write down a very full description of the issue that causes you to be stressed. If yours is a relationship problem, for example, don't just write down, 'We have rows all the time.' Look at when you have rows, over what, how long the situation has been like this, what makes it worse, and what makes it better.

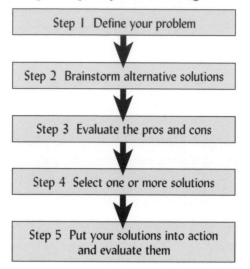

Fig. 7 Steps in problem-solving

You might come up with something like this:

> *We have been arguing ever since Roger has started to work for himself. Most of the arguments are over the fact that I never see him anymore; he works every evening and on the weekend he's too tired to do anything, or he's working. We argue most if I have nothing happening in my life and have to sit at home on my own every evening. We argue less if he makes an effort on the weekends and we do something together.*

Once you have clearly defined your problem, you'll find it's much easier to come up with some solutions to it. Deciding on solutions is Step 2 of the problem-solving technique.

Step 2: Brainstorm alternative solutions

Brainstorming means thinking of as many different solutions to your problem as you possibly can. Don't evaluate them at this stage or be critical of them or try to select the best; just aim to create as many different ones as you can. It doesn't matter if they seem totally off the wall or even unlikely to work. Brainstorming gets your brain thinking laterally and allows you to be more creative about your solutions.

Some of the solutions to the relationship problem could be the following:

Roger to go back to a 9 to 5 job again; leave Roger; take up more interests myself so I won't be left alone on my own so often; Roger to cut back on his work and set aside some time to do things together; Roger to tell me when he's going to be working late so I can decide in advance what I want to do then; start working for myself so that I will be working the same hours as Roger; take in a boarder so that I won't be so lonely in the evenings; have a child so I will be more occupied in my spare time.

After you have brainstormed as many different solutions to your problem as you can, evaluate them. This is Step 3.

Step 3: Evaluate the pros and cons

Write down all of your alternative solutions and look at what's likely to happen in each case. Make a list of both the probable positive consequences if you select each option, and the likely negative outcomes. Often there is no one best solution; most choices we make in life have some negative consequences – it's a matter of which of these you can live with.

Part of your list might look like this:

Option 1: Get Roger to cut back on some of his work
Positive outcomes:
- We would have more time together.
- I would not feel so neglected.
- I would feel I had a say in what happens in our life.
- We would not have so many arguments about not spending time together.
- Roger would be less tired on the weekends and feel more like doing things together.

Negative outcomes:
- We would have slightly less money.
- Roger may feel resentful unless he agrees to this.

Option 2: Take in a boarder so that I won't be so lonely in the evenings
Positive outcomes:
- I would have someone to talk to.

- We will have a little more money.
- We would have fewer arguments about not spending time together.

Negative outcomes:
- It won't mean that Roger and I will spend any more time together.
- The boarder could be someone I don't get on with.
- It could be extra work if I have to do all the cooking and cleaning.
- I don't really want the privacy of my home invaded by someone I don't know.

Option 3: Get involved in more activities outside the relationship
Positive outcomes:
- I won't feel so lonely.
- I won't feel so neglected.
- There should be fewer arguments about not spending time together.
- I'll feel more positive about my life if I have more interesting things in it.
- I'll be a more interesting person and so we will have quality time when we are together.

Negative outcomes:
- I won't spend any more time with Roger; we may even grow apart.

You can see that there is no single solution that is perfect and that all options have some disadvantages.

Step 4: Select one or more solutions

The issue of which option or options you select is really one of values. You need to weigh up your priorities. Ask yourself what's important to you? Put yourself in the shoes of Roger's partner. Is it more important to have a balanced life and quality time in your relationship than to have money? If so, Option 1, getting Roger to cut back on some of his work, may be one that you select. You may also want to look at Option 3, getting involved in more activities yourself, to bring some positive things into your own life and the relationship. If money or companionship is very important to you, you may want to select Option 2 as well and take a chance on not getting on with your boarder.

Step 5: Put your solutions into action and evaluate them
Once you have decided which solutions you'll select, make a plan for when and how you're going to put them into operation.

Try out your solutions for two or three months, which is usually long enough to see whether something is going to work. If you're not happy with the outcome then select some of the other alternatives that you haven't considered, or brainstorm some new ones, or talk to someone else: either discuss it with a friend or get professional advice.

Your Life Plan: Step 2

1. *By the end of this chapter your plan should cover the following: All your problems should be identified as changeable or not able to be changed. Those you can change should be marked with a C. Those you cannot change, mark with a T.*

2. *For those you can change, you will have listed exactly what actions you plan to take to change them, and when and how you will put them into operation.*

3. *Decide what length of time you will devote to trying out your solutions before you evaluate their success.*

4. *Check out whether you need to seek advice or to learn any specific techniques.*

5. *Plan how you will do this.*

Paul's Life Plan: Step 2

After I had finished evaluating my diary, I took the kids out for a walk on the beach – which was something I hadn't done for a long time – and while we were scuffing along through the sand, I said to myself, 'So what do you get from this evaluation? What do you want?' The reply was: 'Change. I want to change. I want to take action.'

Change what you can

I went back to my original list of problems to see what I could do about them. I really looked at each one. Having decided that I was determined to do something, the list suddenly seemed to be less daunting. I looked at it like a challenge instead of a sentence, and even this little change in thought helped. A ripple of energy ran through my brain. Okay, I said, what do you need to do here?

Action plan

- Get the fence repaired. That just means making a couple of phone calls. That's simple.
- Now Don. Squash. What's the problem? The problem is that you don't like playing squash and you've been persuaded into this weekly squash date with Don because that's what the guys do. But what you'd really like to do is lift weights – maybe even go to a pump class, because that looks like fun. It's aerobic and strength work. Call Don and cancel the squash on a permanent basis. Do it cheerfully. Make an appointment at the gym to check out classes.
- Face it, Paul. You did spend too much money on the bathroom, but there's nothing you can do about that now. Forget it.
- As for Dad, on Saturday you're going to go round there with that book you promised to lend him and you're going to ask him about his health.

The two big things I felt I couldn't do anything about right away were my anxiety over my trip to Boston and the perception that something needed fixing in my relationship with Becky. In fact the two things were intertwined, it seemed to me, but I couldn't figure out how exactly. Somewhere at the bottom of it all was my inability to believe in myself. I really didn't think much of myself. I don't know where this came from, but it's coloured all my thinking. I've really been Mr Negative all my life. Up till now, I've hidden it pretty well. But even though, to look at me from the outside, you'd say I was a successful person, I don't actually believe it myself. I'm waiting to be unmasked as an incompetent fool. That's why I can't ever really enjoy anything.

I concluded that there was something quite big and pervasive ruling my life, but I had no idea what the hell it was. It was just a bunch of question marks – all of them hovering over my relationship with Becky. We didn't know what to say to each other. I knew I was going to have to find out how to really talk to her. I mean, we're always talking, but most of the time I don't know if we say what we really think. I knew I had to reconnect with her – establish communication –

and to do that, I was going to have to adjust my attitude.

For several days I was chewing over in my head what I was going to say to Becky. I couldn't figure out where to start. I rehearsed dozens of different speeches and rejected all of them because I thought I sounded like a pathetic, neurotic guy and that when I dumped all this stuff on her, she'd just look at me pityingly, lose whatever respect she had left for me and quietly withdraw even further. And because all of this was spinning around in my mind, I was even more distracted at work. But I recognised what was happening. It was the same old Paul – paralysed by negative thoughts. If I didn't control the way I was thinking, I was never going to be able to communicate effectively with Becky. I said to myself, could you just isolate a positive thought here in all this morass of anxiety? Could you attach a positive thought to the situation with Becky? And, of course, I could – because my fundamental feeling about Becky was that I loved her. I thought: 'She is my wife and I love her.'

When I came home from work, Becky was out in the garden tying up tomato plants. She said hello, but didn't approach me. Why would she? I was usually in a foul temper when I got home and it would take about an hour for me to calm down enough to be civil. I dumped my briefcase and walked over to watch what she was doing. The garden looked great. Becky's really got a green thumb. The vegetable patch was crammed with herbs and salad greens and I wondered when she had planted all these things. Suddenly I heard myself saying, 'I've been hell to live with Beck. I'm trying to figure out why.' And she replied, 'Paul you've been hell to live with. I'd love to know why too.' Then she smiled, which helped a million, and I just started talking to her.

Once I got going, it wasn't too hard. When I heard myself speaking I was amazed at the admissions I was making. That my whole life I had felt inadequate and that was spilling over into my marriage. I didn't believe that she really valued me. Why would she when I didn't value myself? I told her I was convinced that she would wake up one morning and having seen what a jerk I really am, she would take the kids and leave. All my reactions to her were fuelled by jealousy and inadequacy. And then I heard myself saying something – and it wasn't until the words were coming out of my mouth that I realised what my frantic fear about going to Boston had been about: 'The thing is, Becky, I'm in a twist about going away to Boston because, while I'm gone, you're going to find out that life is much better without me. You won't have to put up with my headaches and my moods. And you'll be going to your Spanish classes, and I know you like your teacher a lot, and he'll ask you out for a coffee – and I'll come home to find that you've run away with him to Barcelona or something. I know it sounds crazy, but that's what I've been thinking.'

Becky was stunned at this. She said, 'Paul, I'm not running away to Barcelona with Luis. I'm not even going to have a coffee with him. Darling, you're way out of touch.' I thought, she hasn't called me 'darling' in a long time. But she went on to say that she did think that I didn't care about her and that she was pissed off having to carry the burden of everything because I was so preoccupied by the ongoing drama of my situation at work. Then the kids came home from the neighbour's place and we let the conversation lie. But it was a good start. That evening the atmosphere in the house was a lot better. That night we made a pact that we would communicate better from now on. We agreed that our relationship couldn't take any more of the silent treatment or bottling things up, and that we would remind each other to be more open. I realised how much of my problem about Becky was due to misunderstanding how she felt, and being unable to tell her how I felt.

Summing Up

Step 2: Take action to change what you can
- Decide what you can change and what you cannot.
- Find your solutions, make your plan, decide how and when to evaluate it.
- Extra help: practical and professional advice; problem solving.

Control your thoughts and emotions

Step 3: Change your attitude if you can't change the situation

Our lives are what our thoughts make of them.

MARCUS AURELIUS

Change your thoughts and you change your emotions

Many of life's most painful emotions are caused by events that are as unalterable by human action as the wind, the tide or the sun. What do you do if you cannot take action to solve your problems and get rid of the stress they cause you? It is important to face the fact that there will always be some things in your life that distress you, but which you cannot change, or that you will choose not to change, or that are, by their nature, unchangeable. These will still upset and disturb you; they can make your life as unhappy and out of control as any of those you can alter. Lost loves, betrayals, missed opportunities and ill-considered actions – these are the stuff of our bitterest regrets, but they are not things you can reverse, nor are fears and dreads about what the future holds in store for you.

How can you deal with your feelings about events over which you have no control? Is it inevitable that you remain a victim of them? You may have thought that you couldn't change your emotions, that you were at the mercy of them. That is not so. You can learn to control even your strongest emotions.

You have probably always accepted that you could control your thoughts. If you want to plan your day, you have always known that you could direct your thoughts to construct a schedule. Because your emotions start off as thoughts, you can also learn how to change them.

> *You can learn to control even your strongest emotions.*
> *You do it first by changing your thoughts.*

Change your thoughts and control your stress

Because it is not the events of your life in themselves that disturb you, but rather the view you take of them, you need to have some way of controlling and of changing these perceptions. If you think back to the diagrams in Chapter 1 you can see just how important it is that you have some control over your thoughts. Without them you would have no stress. Without the skill to change your thoughts, you will never control your stress properly. Without this skill, you will never control your life. This chapter is the most crucial in the book, because it tells you how to alter your thoughts and emotions.

Let us be clear here. We are not talking about cutting out the human emotions that are a normal part of the experience of being alive, that fuel growth and self-development and art and literature, nor are we talking about burying your head in the sand and suppressing issues you should address. We are talking about a mechanism for dealing with the pain and despair and fear of being out of control of your life.

> *Without the skill to change your thoughts, you will never*
> *control your stress properly.*

If you direct your thoughts away from the negative, you will still experience pain and sadness and despair, but they will not overpower you. If you have a way of controlling their intensity and duration, you will not experience the terrible sense of impending doom that comes when you can feel life slipping from your grasp.

> *When I knew I was heading for my breakdown, I had this horrifying image in my mind all the time that I was running frantically in sinking sand up the beach, with a tidal wave about to break over my head. It paralysed me, and I could do nothing to avoid what became inescapable.*

Negative thoughts are the beginning of the stress cycle. Altering them will prevent the rest of the cycle from happening. If you don't think the thought, you don't feel the emotion, and you don't produce the physical symptoms of stress. If you don't have the physical symptoms, you don't have any of the breakdown of your organ functions and you don't have the behavioural changes which will get you further into difficulty. Nor will you experience any of the black, paranoid thinking that goes along with prolonged stress and keeps the whole merry-go-round circling.

You have a choice about whether to be stressed or not. Everything in the world can be either changed or regarded differently. You can choose to dwell on things that are unchangeable – guilt and regrets from your past, anxieties and fears about your future, inadequacies in yourself and your present existence – and thereby become unhappy, feel conscience-stricken, or afraid, or depressed, or angry or unconfident. But, in doing so, you are also accepting the burden of additional consequences.

You are choosing to live with long-term, unpleasant and ultimately harmful physical stress symptoms; you are choosing to react much more emotionally to other upsetting events in your life; you are choosing to create far more stress in your life than you have already and to abdicate some of the control over your life that you would otherwise have. Ask yourself whether it is worth it.

> *By being able to change the way you look at the events which distress you, you are also choosing to decide for yourself what kind of quality your life will have.*

Which situations are unchangeable?

You may be asking yourself now how you can identify the unchangeable variety of stress. Obviously you shouldn't ignore a situation which cries out for firm action. Generally, you will have no problem in deciding whether you can change a situation that stresses you if you ask yourself the question, 'What can I do about this?' Usually it is also obvious when no possible action will alter it.

If you are unsure, look through your stress diary now to see which of your sources of stress fit any of the following three categories.

Situations you have chosen not to change

> *The highest possible stage in moral culture is when we recognise that we ought to control our thoughts.*
>
> CHARLES DARWIN

Sometimes the most logical decision you can make is to endure a situation that causes you stress. If you have weighed the pros and cons and decided that the consequences of taking action will be worse than not doing so, there may be nothing else you can do other than to switch off the thoughts your problem generates and view it in a different light. For example, you may dislike your job, but having no job is worse than walking out. Until you find a new job, you need to be able to put up with the stress of the present one.

Or you may be married, no longer in love, and feeling desperately unhappy, but have made a deliberate decision to stay together for your children. You may consider it's better for them to have two parents, and believe that your own needs are less important than theirs for the time being. You cannot change this situation; you have elected to stay in it, you are not happy with it and it stresses you. The more you dwell on it, the more upset about it you will become, and the less tolerable it will be for you. You need to be able to see it differently so it will not torment you.

The past and the future

> *The moving finger writes, and having writ moves on*
> *Not all thy piety and wit can lure it back to cancel half a line,*
> *Nor all thy tears wash out a word of it.*
>
> EDWARD FITZGERALD

The past and the future cannot be changed; you have no life at all if you cannot accept that and live in the present. This does not mean that you should not plan for your future or learn from your past; but it does mean that dwelling on disappointments and regrets, and brooding on fears and forebodings, can destroy your happiness right now.

> *Dwelling on disappointments and regrets, and brooding on fears and forebodings, can destroy your present happiness.*

Yesterday has gone and you cannot rewrite it, but you can create your own hell on earth today by not accepting that. Constantly dwelling on a past where you were unhappy will create stress and depression in your life today, regardless of what else is going on for you.

Once I started to notice the thoughts that made me feel depressed, I realised they weren't about anything that was going on now. They were all about things that had happened to me years ago. It was as though I'd stopped living then and the intervening time had been spent in reliving those terrible times. I felt I'd been marking time for nearly half my life. What a waste! It shattered me!

You would be surprised how many people spend a significant portion of their day reliving times that have been unhappy. Sometimes these recollections reach right back into early childhood. They have kept alive vivid memories of teachers who treated them unfairly, parents who were unkind and critical, friends who let them down. They can quote you chapter and verse.

My eighth birthday party when everyone ran away and hid from me – I'll never forget it, it's just as though it was yesterday.

Or they may relive later losses and disappointments: jobs they missed out on, relationships that disintegrated, or feelings of guilt for sins of omission.

I've never really recovered from my marriage break-up and it's 10 years ago now. A lot of what went on then was my fault. I wish I could turn back the clock and do it all over again differently.

It's pointless to live in the past. Shakespeare said, 'What's gone and what's past help should be past grief'. Even if you cannot change your situation, you can learn to accept it.

It is not only living in the past that can make you stressed and unhappy. Living in the future, especially if it is a future you fear, can be equally frustrating.

You can waste a lot of your life thinking thoughts like, 'What will happen to me when I get old? Who will look after me? How will I support myself?' What is the purpose of this kind of angst, other than to ensure that your life today is flooded with foreboding? It will probably paralyse your ability to provide for your old age, and bring about the thing you most dread.

> *Most of what you fear never happens, and the future can be changed as little as the past.*

If you are the sort of person who lives in fear of the future, your thoughts on other matters may run like this: 'I had better not take the risk and borrow money for a house because if the interest rates go up I might not be able to pay it back.' Or this: 'What will happen if I can't remember all I have learned for this exam? I couldn't bear to fail. What on earth would the family say? What would happen to my career?'

If you hamstring yourself with anxieties like these, at best you will never achieve to your full potential, at worst you will create what you most fear. If you don't buy your house, you may end up homeless at 65. In the exam room, you will undoubtedly drive all you have learned from your head and arrive in a state of blind panic. In your relationship, such bleak speculations will make you depressed, anxious, unconfident and probably not terribly attractive to be around. Your thoughts may become a self-fulfilling prophecy. You are better to eradicate these thoughts entirely from your head.

> *I've been through some terrible things in my life,*
> *and some of them actually happened.*
>
> MARK TWAIN

Putting yourself down

But I do nothing upon myself and yet I am mine own executioner.

JOHN DONNE

Unchangeable stress can also spring from the way in which you think about yourself. Some thinking is essentially self-destructive. If you are dissatisfied with a quality you cannot change, you will create huge unhappiness for yourself by dwelling on it. You may be discontented with the way you look. You may consider you are too tall or too short, or dislike your face or the colour of your skin. Or you may be dissatisfied with what you have achieved in life; you may see yourself as unsuccessful because you don't make enough money. Or you may doubt your ability in certain situations and so avoid them. These are all self-handicapping thoughts. Dwelling on them will cripple your ability to succeed and render you less able to control the parts of your life you can control. You cannot change your height and many of your other physical characteristics and you cannot make yourself more successful or confident while you are telling yourself that you are not.

You're also opening the door to criticism from other people if you dwell on your failings.

You will be a happier, more successful and more confident person if you stop obsessing about the qualities you do not like and focus instead on the ones you do like about yourself.

He who undervalues himself is justly undervalued by others.

WILLIAM HAZLITT

How to control what you cannot change

If you cannot change a situation, you can always change your attitude to it. The only way to handle the stress you create by thinking about situations you cannot alter is to alter those thoughts themselves. You need to be able to change the way you see the situation and produce in yourself an attitude to it that is positive, or is one that you can live with.

To do this, you need a mechanism for switching off the thoughts that upset you and replacing them with a calming thought. If you direct yourself to think positive or coping thoughts, you will produce emotions in line with those views. As you think, so you will feel.

Shakespeare is not the only person to have expressed this belief. Many famous people have come to this conclusion and maybe it's one of the reasons they have succeeded in life.

Earlier the point was made that psychologists have recently established, scientifically, what lay people have known for years: that positive, optimistic thinking is helpful. If the effects of being optimistic were limited to making you feel better, the research would be less surprising, though still interesting, but the effects of positive thinking go far beyond simply making you feel happier. As you saw in Chapter 4, investigations have now shown that optimism also helps people to manage their stress and to reach their goals more effectively, and to live longer.

How do you think you will feel if, instead of thinking 'What will happen when I'm old?', you think, 'I will make sure I live to the full today!' Your emotional state will change from one of dread and fear to optimism and enjoyment, and you will find you have the drive and the confidence to make the best decisions for your future.

If you think, 'I wish I wasn't so short. I'm always being overlooked', you will feel unconfident and insecure, and you probably will be overlooked. If you think instead, 'Napoleon was short and look where he got. It's my personality that's important!', you will feel confident and in control, and even if you don't end up an emperor, you are likely to win your battles and to reach your goals.

Sometimes it's not realistically possible to be positive about your circumstances. If your partner has left you for someone else, the attitude you take will more likely be philosophical than positive. If you think, 'How will I get by without her? My life is in ruins', you will feel devastated and powerless. If instead you think, 'Be calm, I will get on with my life', your pain will be reduced and you will be more in control of your situation.

If you direct yourself to think positive or coping thoughts, you will produce emotions in line with those views.

How can you change your thinking to become more calm and peaceful and confident? What is the secret? If it was so easy, wouldn't you have done it already?

There is nothing either good or bad but thinking makes it so.
WILLIAM SHAKESPEARE

Switch it off: thought-stopping

The easiest and by far the most effective way you can change your thoughts and control your emotions is a technique called thought-stopping. A method of controlling negative thoughts and feelings by switching off thoughts that stress you, thought-stopping is also a form of positive thinking, because it allows you to replace your negative thoughts with coping or positive ones.

'Positive thinking' is a term that's used a lot in self-improvement books. Generally these books do not teach you how to think positively, they just say, 'Do it!' But that is not enough. What these books do not explain is how you stop thinking the negative thoughts first; and that is essential.

> *Being able to stop or switch off your negative thoughts is a vital prerequisite to thinking positively, to controlling your stress and, ultimately, to having control over your world.*

If you can't stop your negative thinking first, all the positive thinking in the world will do you no good, because negative thoughts will override and overwhelm your positive thoughts. Negative thoughts, under normal circumstances, win hands down in the battle for the mind. Why is this?

The power of negative thinking

Negative thoughts are self-generating. Once the stress reaction starts, the depressant activity of the stress chemicals causes more and more upsetting thoughts to crowd into your brain, which makes you feel increasingly emotionally distressed. Positive thoughts, unfortunately, do not operate like this. They are much less self-generating.

The power of negative thinking undoubtedly arose from the need to survive. The process of natural selection results in the survival of those individuals best adapted to the prevailing environmental conditions. Natural selection produced the fight/flight mechanism, which once was more important for survival than it is now. When you lived in a cave, negative thoughts were part of what made the fight/flight mechanism work and ensured you a long life. Positive thoughts were not so important. Back in the early history of humans, moving away from harmful objects was more likely to result in survival of the species.

Now, of course, negative thoughts are not helpful to the same extent in survival, or in running your life effectively. In fact, negative thoughts are pretty counterproductive; certainly they are counterproductive to living a high quality life.

Learning to thought-stop

Step 1
Select from your stress diary a thought that upsets you and which you have identified as being about a situation you cannot change. It doesn't really matter which thought you choose, because once you have learned to switch off one thought using this technique, you will understand the process and be able to apply it to any other thought that troubles you, but do select a very upsetting thought. If you prove to yourself that you can become less emotional about this problem, then dealing with any other will seem easy and you will start to have faith in your own ability to control your emotions, your stress and your attitude to the world.

Step 2
Write down the thought you have chosen and look at it carefully. Ask yourself these questions: What attitude to this situation would I rather have? What is the attitude I can live with? Or, what is a positive attitude I can believe?

What you are looking for here is an alternative thought or a replacement thought for the one that troubles you. When you switch off a thought that produces a negative emotion, you need to put in its place a positive or a coping thought, one that will not upset you but will calm you and make you feel more in control. Be realistic, however – your replacement thought cannot be something that you would not believe.

Maybe you are someone who dwells on guilt and inadequacies. You feel guilty about not meeting your parents' expectations in life because you became a salesperson rather than the lawyer they expected. So you identify the thought that upsets you as: 'I have not done what the family expected of me in life'; it would be foolish to think 'I did do what the family expected of me', because you did not. You would be better to replace that thought with something like: 'I did what was right for me' or 'Their expectations were unrealistic'; or 'People need to live their own lives'; or 'I need to be true to myself'.

The briefer the thought, the better, just as long as it incorporates your meaning and your intent. If, for example, you were to write down: 'My parents were unrealistic in their expectations of me; they tried to force me to be the kind of person they wanted to be themselves because they felt they had not fulfilled their own expectations', this may be true, but you will not remember it when you have switched off the thought that upsets you. You require a briefer thought. You will notice when you write down the thoughts that upset you that they are usually very brief too. The following are typical thoughts that have upset others and typical replacement thoughts they have used.

> George blamed me for things going wrong between us.
> *The blame was not mine. I really tried.*
> Oh God, I'm going to mess this up.
> *Be calm and you will be fine.*
> Maybe she doesn't love me.
> *You have to trust her.*
> I can't stand this damn noise!
> *They're just being kids and I love them.*

Sometimes you may find that a situation requires you to take some action as well as changing your attitude. You may have decided that you hate your job and would best solve your problem by leaving your job in six months time, but you are still bothered because you have not yet carried out your plan to leave. When that is the case, you are better to switch off the thoughts that cause your anxiety and say to yourself something like: 'I have a plan' or 'I have made a decision' or 'I know what I have to do', or 'Relax: it's only another six months'.

Step 3

Write down your replacement thought. This will become your new attitude to what stresses you.

Now you need to establish it in your mind. You can either teach yourself how to do this, or you can ask a friend to be your tutor and teach it to you by reading aloud the instructions below. Using a tutor is easier. But both sets of instructions are included here.

An overview of thought-stopping

Here is a brief description of the thought-stopping process. It helps to get an idea of what it involves before you learn it step by step.

First you will voluntarily bring to mind the negative thought you have selected to change. As soon as it starts to come into your head, either you or your tutor will shout STOP! You will see that the thought totally disappears from your mind, as does any emotion accompanying it. Then you are going to say aloud the replacement or calming thought. You will move by a series of gradual stages to the point where you are carrying out the whole procedure in your head. In the beginning, though, it helps if you verbalise it.

It is useful to know that the real key to switching off unwanted negative thoughts is to stop them when they are just starting to take form in your head by putting a block in between the thought and its subsequent emotions. If you allow the thoughts to take full form in your head and then dwell on them, not only do you feel emotionally upset but you set off the stress cycle. It is then harder to switch off the thoughts. You can still eliminate them, but it's not as easy, because they give rise to more negative thoughts.

Here you go!

Learning thought-stopping with a tutor

Step 1

Tutor: *'I want you to just start to get into your head the thought that upsets you. As soon as it starts to come, put your finger up so I know it's there.'*

As soon as the student raises a finger, the tutor says very loudly:
    'STOP! What are you going to say instead?'

Student says the replacement or calming thought.

Tutor: *'You need to practise this, so we'll do it four more times while I say STOP! Then I will get you to say STOP!'*

Repeat Step 1 four times more. After the first of these four times:

Tutor: *'When I said STOP!, did the upsetting thought disappear?'*

If the reply is yes, proceed with the other three.

Troubleshooting

If the thought does not disappear with the first STOP!, the student has probably not raised a finger early enough. The STOP! needs to be said when the thought is just starting to formulate itself, but before it has made the student feel negative emotionally and set off the stress cycle.

A second reason for the negative thought remaining may be that the student has not focused their thinking actively into the replacement thought. Instruct them to think strongly about the calming thought. It helps to get a visual image of what they are saying when they speak the replacement thought.

> *My replacement thought was 'I want to be happy'. I didn't actually plan it, but when I said it a picture came into my head of a time one morning when I was a kid. We were all going to the beach for a picnic – I couldn't wait to get there, I had a new boogie board and I could see those blue sparkling waves. The sun was hot on my back, the cicadas were singing and the world was full of promise and hope. That was a great replacement thought for me.*

If the student still has difficulty getting rid of the negative thought, even when they are thinking strongly about the replacement thought, instruct them to move their eyes to a different part of the room when you say STOP! This is very effective at breaking the train of the upsetting thought.

Do not move onto the next step until you can make the negative thought disappear by saying STOP!

Step 2

Tutor: *'Now you are going to say STOP! First, I want you to think the upsetting thought, then I want you to say STOP! to it as loudly as you can. You need to put some force into this, because effort will break the train of your thought. Then say out loud the calming thought'.*

Student does Step 2.

Tutor: *'When you said STOP!, did the upsetting thought disappear?'*

If it did not disappear, the student probably did not say STOP! at the very beginning of the thought, but let it get well established and set off the stress cycle. In this case, troubleshoot as for Step 1 and ask them to say STOP! to the upsetting thought as many times as necessary for the thought to go.

Repeat Step 2 four times.

Step 3

Tutor: *'This time I want you to still say the STOP! out loud but I want you to think both the upsetting thought and the calming thought. You are getting nearer now to the point where everything goes on in your head. As you think the replacement thought, I want you to breathe in and to breathe out. When you do this you will find you are quite relaxed. Remember, only the STOP! is out loud now, everything else is in your head.'*

The student does Step 3. The tutor reminds them to breathe in and out as they are thinking the replacement thought by saying 'Breathe' as soon as they have said STOP!

Repeat Step 3 four times.

Step 4

Tutor: *'This time I want you to do everything in your head. This is the final procedure. Think the upsetting thought. Think STOP! with as much effort as you can. Think the calming thought and breathe while you do.'*

You may find it helps to have visual or auditory images of both the calming thought and the STOP! while you do this. Sometimes people say things like, 'I see a big red stop sign come down, or it's like the television went off, or I hear a voice shouting STOP! Whatever works for you, use it.

Student does Step 4.

My upsetting thought was 'God, you're a fool, you've made a real idiot of yourself again'. When I thought STOP, I heard a big clap of thunder and I switched into: 'I'm a good person, my kids love me', and I forgot about the faux pas.

My stressful thought was 'I could lose my job in the restructuring'. When I said STOP, I saw this bright red bulldozer push a huge pile of mud over a cliff. The mud was all the anxiety that had been clogging up in my head. Then I thought, 'I want to be calm and competent', and I saw myself at work, doing one of the things I know I do really well.

Practise Step 4 another four times.

You may notice that it gets more difficult to generate the original negative thought as you keep stopping it. That's to be expected. You are actually weakening that thought every time you stop it. You will also notice that by the time you have learned the full process of switching off the upsetting thought, it does not upset you as much. That means you have started to change your attitude to it permanently.

Teaching yourself thought-stopping

First, read through the instructions for learning with a tutor. Note particularly the section on troubleshooting, because if you have difficulties, this section explains how you can solve them.

Step 1

Start to get into your head the thought that upsets you. As soon as it starts to come, shout STOP, then say your replacement thought out loud.

If the upsetting thought disappears from your head when you shout STOP!, repeat Step 1 ten more times.

If it does not disappear when you shout STOP, look at the section on troubleshooting and follow the instructions there. Do not progress on to Step 2 until you can make the negative thought disappear by saying STOP! to it. When you can make it disappear repeat Step 1 ten more times.

Step 2

This time you will still say the STOP! out loud but you will think both the upsetting thought and the calming thought. Remember, only the STOP! is out loud now, everything else is in your head.

Start to get into your head the thought that upsets you. As soon as it starts to come, shout STOP, then think your replacement thought.

Repeat Step 2 five more times.

Step 3

Step 3 is almost the same as Step 2. You will still be saying the STOP! out loud, and you will think both the upsetting thought and the calming thought. But in addition, this time, as you think the replacement thought, you will breathe in and breathe out. When you do this you will find that it relaxes you. Remember, only the STOP! is out loud now. Everything else is in your head. Breathe in and out as you are thinking the replacement thought.

Start to get into your head the thought that upsets you. As soon as it starts to come, shout STOP, then think your replacement thought and breathe in and out.

Repeat Step 3 five more times.

Step 4

This time everything is in your head, nothing is out loud. This is the final procedure. You may find that it helps to have visual or auditory images of both the calming thought and the STOP! while you do this. Check back to Step 4 of the instructions with a tutor on page 156 for examples of the kind of visual images or auditory images other people have selected.

Think the upsetting thought. Think STOP! with as much effort as you can. Think the replacement thought and breathe in and out.

Repeat Step 4 five more times.

The number of times suggested for you to practise each step is arbitrary. It is usually more than sufficient for most people, but you may need to practise more often before you feel totally in control of your negative thinking. Do so if you need to. Decide for yourself how many times you need to repeat each step so that you are able to stop the negative thoughts before they upset you.

How to use thought-stopping

Now you have learned how to thought-stop on one thought, you will be able to short circuit the process with other thoughts. You will probably be able to switch off mentally, i.e. at Step 4, any other thought that upsets you, without having to go through the other three stages.

As soon as you find yourself thinking a thought that upsets you – one you have identified as being about a situation which is unchangeable – think STOP! and follow it with a positive replacement thought. Don't forget the positive replacement thought; you will weaken the negative thought if you stop it, but you won't change your attitude to the situation unless you replace the negative with a positive thought.

> *As soon as you find yourself thinking a thought that upsets you think STOP! and follow it with a positive replacement thought.*

You may find it's useful to pick yourself a replacement or a calming thought that you can use with any thought that troubles you. This can be a generic thought like 'Be calm, I want to be in control of my life!', although many people say they prefer to select a specific positive thought for each negative one.

What happens if you cannot switch off other stressful thoughts mentally? If you have a particularly strong negative thought which you find difficult to switch off at Step 4, select the right replacement thought and go through all four steps with it. You will find that this weakens it enough to be manageable.

If it continues to come back in its weakened form, just continue to switch it off, call it up and switch it off, say 50 times. Remember that you can only think about one thing at a time, so distract yourself after this by thinking about something else, something that gives you pleasure, or busy yourself in some other activity to take your mind off it.

What happens if your thoughts don't stay switched off?

There are two reasons upsetting thoughts may return to trouble you after you have followed the suggestions above. The first is that the problem is one for which you should have taken some action and not switched off. The second is that you have chosen the wrong replacement thought.

1. When you make a wrong decision and attempt to switch off something that really requires action, often it will not stay switched off. It's as though your brain or some instinct of self-preservation is telling you, 'Hey, you have made the wrong choice. Do something!' The problem keeps coming back to you and you will find that your original negative thoughts will not leave you alone. If this is what has happened to you, go back to Chapter 6, and work it through from there. Decide what action you need to take to solve your problem.

2. If your original negative thought keeps returning and you are quite clear there is no action you can take to change the situation, you will find it's probably because the way you have told yourself to look at your situation is not convincing to you. The attitude you finally take to a problem that cannot be changed has to be one that you believe and one that you can accept.

Here is the mental process gone through by someone who experienced this difficulty:

John and I had been together for six years. He was the only man that I had ever thought I would like to spend the rest of my life with, so when I found out that he had been having an affair with his secretary and that he wanted to leave me and live with her, my whole world stopped.

After we separated I was in a state of shock for a long time. I don't know how long really. Then, friends persuaded me to go for counselling. My psychologist taught me thought-stopping and it was very effective when I learnt it in his consulting room. I learned it around dealing with my fears that I would never be in another relationship, but when I got home and realised how much of my anguish was actually caused by thinking about John and wishing we were still together, I decided to thought-stop on him. It didn't seem to work. It stopped the thoughts temporarily, but they still came back. What I was saying to myself when I thought about John was: 'I don't love him'. What I realised in very short order was, of course, that I did still love him, I rang my psychologist and we talked over what was the appropriate thing to say and I came up with two replacement thoughts. One of them was 'I could never trust him again' and the other was 'I want to get on with my life'. These two thoughts were a true reflection of my feelings. They gave me the power and the motivation to pick up my life and to put it back together again. I didn't look back from that time on.

If you're sure your problem is not one that requires action, and you're confident that you have chosen the right replacement thought, but you still find it difficult to switch off your thoughts, or they don't stay switched off, you may be depressed. When you are depressed all your thoughts are likely to be overwhelmingly negative, you switch off one thought and it's instantly replaced with another, just as negative, or you can be too exhausted and unmotivated to persevere with thought-stopping. If this is the case, don't struggle, talk to your doctor about antidepressants and come back to your thought-stopping once the antidepressants have taken effect.

Depression can interfere with thought-stopping.

Confiding your troubles

One often calms one's grief by recounting it.

PIERRE CONNIELLE

Sometimes all you need to do in order to change your thoughts about situations that upset you is to talk things over with someone who has a different perspective on them. If you are stressed you will have tunnel vision; you will not think of all the options and you will not see things clearly or objectively. Problems will seem huge and unmanageable even when they are relatively trivial.

If you want to confide in someone, make sure it is a person you trust, and make sure you are open with them, that your communication is assertive. Use 'I' statements: 'This is how I see the situation ... This is how I feel about it', so that they really understand how big the problem is for you and how it is affecting you.

At times you don't even really need the advice that they will give you. You just need to be able to explore all the possible angles and ways of looking at your problem. By doing this you may be able to come to an attitude to your problem that you can live with. Confiding is rather like finding the appropriate replacement thought when you are thought-stopping, but not having to switch off the thought. By the time you have explored all the angles of your problem, you have figured out how you want to see it and have changed your attitude about it, to one that no longer upsets you.

A book by James Pennebaker, an American psychologist, claims that people who put their most troubling experiences into language, either by confiding in someone else or simply by writing them down and never showing them to anyone, are profoundly relieved of the stress symptoms in their bodies and feel happier. Based on his research with people who had experienced a wide range of personal traumas – from abusive childhoods to fighting in Vietnam – Pennebaker found that people who confided their troubling experiences, whether it was to a friend, to a partner, in the confessional or in a diary, could be emotionally and physically relieved of the stress caused by their traumas.

> *Confiding your troubling experiences can relieve you*
> *of the stress they cause.*

As you're aware by now, it is not just 'letting it all hang out' that helps with confiding, it is the making sense of it. It is the changing of your attitude to your problems, the thinking of them in a different way. If you confide in someone, but don't think about what you're saying, it won't work. Or, if you think about it in the wrong way, it won't work. If while you're confiding, you're thinking 'Poor me, I've had such a terrible life, I'll never get over it', you'll feel even worse than when you started. The more you can talk about your experiences, make sense of them and integrate them into something that you can understand and come to terms with, the better you will feel. If you sit down and sort out the meaning and purpose that things have for you, then you start to feel that you are in control of them, you then feel better and, of course, you cope better.

Positive thinking

A third set of techniques useful to change your attitude to things that stress you centre around positive thinking. The replacement thoughts that you use after you thought-stop are positive, but this is not exactly what is meant here. Positive thinking involves an active search for the good things that happen in your day as a counterbalance to obsessing about those that are not good.

> *Positive thinking involves an active search for the good things that happen.*

When you engage in positive thinking, you focus on the happinesses, the joys, the delights, the successes in your life. You hunt them out and dwell on them as much as you dwell on the worries, frustrations, the failures and the sadness. Because your brain can only think about one thing at a time, if you concentrate on what goes well in your day, you are going to feel optimistic and positive. If you concentrate on what goes wrong, you will feel low and down. And because positive thoughts also alter your biochemistry in a positive way they dilute the depressing and physically harmful effects of the chemicals you release when you're concentrating on what goes wrong in your day.

When do you need to do this? Anyone can benefit from concentrating on the positive, but positive thinking is particularly helpful if you have had a lot of stress in your past. Earlier you learned how a history of stress in your younger life can leave you a pessimist rather than an optimist. Perhaps you wonder why you never feel happy even when there seems nothing wrong in your life today. If your life has been stressful and unhappy in the past, chances are that you have learned to focus primarily on the bad things that happen to you and to discount or ignore anything positive. If 10 things happen in your day and one is bad, it has been a bad day; you ignore the other nine. You don't see the world clearly. You see it through dark glasses, certainly not through rose-tinted ones.

This imbalance in perception can also happen when you are going through a prolonged period of stress. You can find it almost impossible to feel happy or to see that anything in your life is good. Although people may think that a lot of your life is fine and objectively you may agree that not everything is wrong, emotionally you feel that nothing is right. Concentrating on the positive events in your day can reverse this imbalance in your thinking. You can retrain yourself to see the glass as half full not as half empty.

How to think positively

Note some positive events

When you kept your stress diary you took notes on things that upset you throughout your day. In the same way, now take notes on things that are positive, events that give you pleasure, joy or happiness. Don't write a lot, just a line or two, enough so that you can remember again what it was and how you felt about it. As you did with recording negative events, make sure that you write things down as they happen, because you will forget them by the end of the day. Keep a notebook or a piece of paper and pen on you.

When you have written down what happened, don't just put it out of your mind but think about it for a while, dwell on it. You don't have to write down only major events – they can be quite small; but if you spend time thinking about them, they will be very powerful. They will change your thinking and your emotions, and they will turn off the stress cycle.

Talk about the positive events

Read your list every time you add something to it, and at the end of the day see if you can talk about it to someone.

A good idea is to institute a 'What good things happened to you today?' regular conversation over the dinner table. You can change the mood of the whole family by doing this. Or talk about it with your partner or with a friend. If someone says to you, 'How was your day?', don't just say 'lousy' or 'okay', itemise the good things for them. If you do this over a few weeks, you will become far more optimistic and far more attuned to seeing what is good about your life. You will develop a more balanced view of your existence, and you will become less stressed and more laid back over the bad things in it. You will enjoy your life better and you will have a greater sense of control over it.

Here is one person's list – these incidents covered about three hours only.

- It's a beautiful day, the sky is clear and blue and I've just heard the first cicada of the summer. Feel elated.
- Thought I would get trouble from the insurance company and would have to take time off work and go in and fill out the claim form, but they said they would fax it to me. Relief.
- Heard a bird singing, sounded like a shining cuckoo. Uplifted.
- Robert said he was very impressed by my report. Felt good about all the effort.

- Had a conversation with Sean. He thanked me for ringing him; he was pleased to hear from me. He gave me some good news – they may be coming over for Christmas. Looking forward to that.
- Got asked to a party at Bonnie and John's next Saturday night. Looking forward to that – enjoy them and their friends.
- Barbara (daughter) rang and says she's happy. Felt happy and relieved.
- I'm pleased with the way the kitchen looks now it's painted. Pleasure – satisfaction at selecting the right colours.
- My hair looks good today. Gives me confidence.
- The roses on the trellis look wonderful, very healthy, the pink fading into cream is spectacular. Feel uplifted.

Your Life Plan: Step 3
1. *Make a list of all thoughts you've been thinking that are about situations which distress you, but which you cannot change.*
2. *Decide for each of these the attitude to that situation you would rather have.*
3. *Write down for each the replacement thought that will most calm you.*
4. *Teach yourself thought-stopping.*
5. *Spend about five minutes thought-stopping on each of the thoughts listed in 1 above. If those come up again later on, thought-stop on them too.*
6. *Continue recording distressing thoughts you cannot change and thought-stop on them as they arise.*
7. *Decide whether there is something in your life that you need to confide or get off your chest.*
8. *Decide how you will disclose this: to a friend, or by writing it down.*
9. *Teach yourself positive thinking: keep notes on all events, large and small, which bring you joy, happiness, hope, confidence etc. Dwell on them and discuss them.*

Paul's Life Plan: Step 3

When we were getting into bed the night after our conversation in the garden, Becky said, 'Paul, I can reassure you until the cows come home, but will it do any good? You make me feel kind of useless. Like nothing I say can buoy you up. You'll just never believe it because you're so down on yourself, and that's exhausting. I wish you would believe it. You're a good man and I love you. Does that mean anything to you at all? Is there any point in my even saying it?'

And she was right. Because even as she was saying the words 'You're a good man', I was flinching internally. My automatic mental response was: 'No, I'm not. I'm a horrible person.' That's when I decided that I was going to learn thought-stopping to try to reprogram myself.

Thought-stopping

I looked back through my stress diary and selected from the abundant examples a thought that upset me, which was: 'The people in Boston will be furious when they see this financial report.' I figured that the replacement thought I needed was: 'Be calm, you've done nothing wrong.'

After everyone had gone to bed and the house was quiet, I sat down in the living room and thought: 'The people in Boston will be furious ...' Before I could complete the sentence, I cried out 'Stop!' and said: 'Be calm. You've done nothing wrong.' I did this about a dozen times, concentrating hard. After a while I got into the swing of it. By the time I had said 'Stop!' two or three times I was expecting the thought to disappear – and it did, because I couldn't hold the two things in my mind at one time.

I went through all the steps. Finally I did the whole thing silently.

I found this technique invaluable. For the personal put-downs I dished out to myself all the time I used the phrase, 'I'm a good man and Becky loves me'. For all the other things that made me anxious I decided to use an all-purpose phrase, which was: 'Be calm, you can handle this'. I found myself using thought-stopping several times a day. And each time I did it, I got a little surge of relief at switching off the negative thought. It really helped me to calm down.

Positive thinking

The other technique that worked for me was positive thinking. With the issue of going to Boston, for instance, I told myself: 'It's just a temporary thing. You'll be there for five days only. That's nothing. And you do have the skills to handle it.' But I also tried to find positive things that occurred during the day. Before I went to sleep at night, I asked myself to run through a mental list of 10 positive things that I had experienced. At first I had difficulty collecting enough positives, because I wasn't looking at the details of my day. But I started to take notes and then I learned to really look for them, even if it was something as small as finding a good parking space or hearing a song I like on the car radio or enjoying going to bed in freshly laundered sheets. This kind of thinking also made me feel somehow more connected with life. When you perceive your life as one long crisis, there's no space to appreciate little things.

Summing Up

Step 3: Your life is what your thoughts make of it
- If you can't change a situation, you can change your attitude to it.
- Decide what you cannot change: the past and the future.
- Change other causes of unhappiness: self-criticisms, pessimism.
- How you can change your attitude: thought-stopping.
- Other ways to change your thinking: confiding, positive thinking.

Keep fit and be happy

Step 4: Exercise

*Those who think that they have not time for bodily
exercise will sooner or later have to find time for illness.*
THE EARL OF DERBY

To live a normal life without exercise in today's world is, for most people, like running the water into your bath without ever pulling out the plug. Eventually it's going to overflow. There is no way you can manage the day-to-day stress of life in the twenty-first century and have your life under control unless you exercise. That sounds a radical statement, but if you look for a minute at what exercise does, you will understand why it is also a truthful statement.

Stop the stress cycle

What does exercise do for stress? How can exercise reverse the build-up of stress? Exercise fulfils the function that nature intended when the fight/flight mechanism first evolved. Instead of rushing off to fight the bear or fleeing from it, you should do a good workout at the gym, or jump into the swimming pool for a few laps, or go for a half hour's run. Why is this?

When you're stressed, the blood withdraws from the surface of your body and concentrates more heavily in the central part of your body, where the stress chemicals activate your organs to produce the pounding heart, sleeplessness and other physical symptoms of stress. When you exercise, your heart rate increases and this blood is forced into your muscles, skin and extremities. Exercise gives the muscles of your arms and legs the energy your internal organs don't need. If you don't exercise, the stress chemicals don't go anywhere. Your liver metabolises a little of them but most of them remain in your bloodstream energising all your internal organs. You may have experienced the way in which a good run gets your circulation going. That truly is what happens. As well as clearing your body of the build-up of stress hormones and chemicals, and stopping all your physical symptoms of stress, it also arrests further stress, at least for a while, because it has removed the chemicals that cause you to think more depressing, negative and paranoid thoughts.

> *Exercise clears your body of the build-up of stress hormones*
> *and chemicals, stops physical symptoms of stress,*
> *and arrests further stress for a while.*

Start the neurotransmitters and endorphins

Moderate aerobic exercise has three other important effects on your brain which enhance your life.

Producing neurotransmitters

First, exercise encourages the production of noradrenaline or norepinephrine and of serotonin, two of the chemicals involved in neural transmission. These are two of the neural transmitters that make you feel 'up'. People who are under stress for a long time show very low levels of noradrenaline, but studies have shown that a regular exercise program soon leads to an increase of noradrenaline and of serotonin and, from that, to an improvement in mood.

Producing beta-endorphins

Second, exercise greatly increases your body's production of beta-endorphins. Beta-endorphins are one of the endorphin family. Endorphins are amino acids which are neurotransmitters, that is, they are involved in the transmission of information in the brain – but they have an added function. They are one of the body's naturally occurring opiates; they relieve pain by suppressing the signals that transmit pain. They are also mood elevators, with positive, confidence-inducing effects that also counter the depressive action of the stress chemicals.

If you are not familiar with the term endorphin, you may know them as 'natural morphines' which produce the effect of 'runner's high'. Chapter 9 picks up again the subject of chemicals released by the brain which give you this natural high.

I could not survive without exercise! To be frank, I really hate exercising, but I couldn't live my life without it. It does wonderful things for me. I think I'm by nature an indolent and sluggish person, but I know that when I'm feeling down or upset in any way, if I go and do some exercise, the world will become balanced for me again.

Examine carefully your mood or your state of mind before your exercise and after. Convince yourself that you do see the world differently at these times. You won't get a high like the altered state of consciousness when you're drinking or using drugs, but your view of the world will be clear, positive and unbiased by self-doubts. You won't think in a paranoid or suspicious way, you will be confident of your ability to tackle your problems, and you will rise to meet your challenges. You will also be more creative in your thinking.

Improve your learning

The moment my legs begin to move, my thoughts begin to flow.
DAVID HENRY THOREAU

The third important effect of exercise was revealed in recent neuroscientific research which suggests that exercise will not only improve your mood but will boost your brain's capacity and ability to learn. According to Dr John Ratey, Clinical Associate Professor of Psychiatry at Harvard Medical School, exercise increases both blood flow and the levels of brain cell growth hormones. These spur cell growth. Other neurobiological research shows that physical activity also increases the number of brain cells in the hippocampus, which is involved in memory, and that learning improves with exercise.

One study that showed the effects of regular exercise on mental ability was carried out at Purdue University in the United States. Participants in the study were given psychological tests at the beginning, to measure their decision-making abilities. Half of them were then put on a fitness program for six months, while the other half remained unfit. After six months of regular exercise, those participants who exercised improved their decision-making skills by 60 percent more than the group who took no exercise.

> *If I'm going to do something difficult, something that I need to be on top of, a situation where I need to be very calm and clear in my thinking, I'll always exercise beforehand. In my job I do a lot of presentations to prospective clients. We're usually in competition with other companies who're tendering for the same work. It's quite a cut-throat scene. I always go to the gym before I get into the boardroom. If I don't, I'm likely to get anxious, freak out, forget my information, go blank – any of those things. If I have been to the gym first and they get the knives out, there is no way they can rattle me; I see the traps they're setting and I'm able to come across as calm, professional and rational, not as a gibbering incompetent.*

◆ Exercise helps produce the neural transmitters that make you feel good.

◆ It increases the production of beta-endorphins, which relieve pain and lift moods.

◆ It can boost your brain's capacity and ability to learn.

Additional benefits of exercise

Exercise has further benefits that can add to you feeling in control of your life. When health professionals investigate why people exercise, the same five reasons come up time and again:

1. Better health and fitness

You can see that, by cutting your stress level, exercise helps to protect you from the stress-related disorders of Chapter 1. There is also evidence that endorphins strengthen your immune system. Even without the other stress management steps, you will keep better health mentally and physically in all ways if you exercise, and you will live longer.

A study at Duke University Medical Centre in the United States, published in 2000, which looked at mental health issues, found that regular exercise was as effective as antidepressants in combating depression. Dr James Blumenthal and his colleagues gave one of three treatments to people diagnosed with depression: 30 minutes aerobic exercise three times a week; the antidepressant Zoloft; or a combination of the two. At the end of four months all three groups reported similar results: a significant drop in their levels of depression. Interestingly, though, six months later, the people who had been successfully treated with aerobic exercise only were the least likely to have become depressed again. Eight percent of those who exercised saw depression symptoms return compared with 38 percent of those taking drugs, and 31 percent of those who both took drugs and exercised.

Blumenthal suggested that one reason for the exercise working better than the drugs may have been because people gained a sense of control over their lives that those taking drugs could not match. He considered that instead of thinking 'I took an antidepressant and got better', people may have thought 'I was dedicated and worked hard with the exercise program: it wasn't easy but I beat this depression'. Other studies have found that regular exercise may also help people with anxiety or panic disorders and substance abuse disorders, and that it can play a role in increasing work performance for people with Attention Deficit Disorder. There is even suggestive evidence that exercise may be a help to those with schizophrenia, although more studies are needed to confirm this finding.

> *Exercise will protect you from the physical effects of prolonged stress and will prolong your life.*

It seems that exercise will also protect you from the physical effects of prolonged stress and will prolong your life. A 10-year study in Norway looked at the levels of physical activity in over 40,000 women aged 50 and over. None of these women had had a stroke at the beginning of the study. As the years passed, those who did die from strokes were those who exercised least, regardless of their age. The researchers concluded that regular physical activity for middle aged and elderly women reduces the risk of dying from a stroke by about 50 percent. Regular exercise is also known to reduce your risk of heart disease and certain types of cancer.

Lesley Kenton, in her book *Ageless Aging*, quotes a Canadian study by two researchers, Terence Kavanagh and Roy Shepherd, of older athletes, some as old as 90, which established that regular exercise delays ageing. These older athletes showed significantly fewer signs of ageing than the average person of the same age. After you reach 45 you are likely to lose height at the rate of half an inch every 10 years. These athletes had lost less than half that much. They also had less body fat, more muscle and better heart and lung functioning than people of the same age who had not exercised regularly. In addition, their bodies looked younger and stronger than their years.

Many of the diseases that come with old age are not due to age itself, but to lack of use. Researchers now think that as much as 50 percent of the physical decline that comes with age is due to lack of use and can be reversed with exercise. If you keep your body in good working order, these disorders will bypass you.

2. Improved appearance

Exercise not only tones your muscles but it increases your metabolic rate and cuts your appetite at the same time. If you're trying to lose weight you'll find you want less to eat and your body is using up what you do eat faster.

3. Enjoyment

People also exercise for enjoyment. In fact you're not likely to stick at your exercise program unless you find something you can enjoy about it. One way you can get a sense of challenge and enjoyment from your exercise program is by increasing its difficulty and by varying the activities you tackle.

4. Social activity

You can meet new people and strengthen existing friendships through exercise. You're meeting people who share a similar interest, you can compare notes on your progress and you're more likely to feel committed to your exercise program if others are involved. When you exercise with other people you generally enjoy the experience more, whether it's a team sport you're playing or just working out with a partner.

5. Psychological benefits

These are many and varied. You may exercise for the enjoyment of the mood elevation and clarity of thought brought about by endorphin release; the competition and the winning; or, by improving your performance, you may enjoy seeing yourself as an athlete. Or you may value having the space to be alone with yourself. This last is a strong motive for many runners.

The need for exercise

Even if you carry out the other four stress management steps – recognise what upsets you; change what you can; switch off what you can't; and do things you enjoy – you will still need to exercise.

When you solve the problems that affect you and switch off the things that can't be changed by taking a different attitude to them, there is a time lag between your doing that and the firing of the stress reaction. Even if you problem-solve and switch off really assiduously, a certain amount of the stress hormones and chemicals are released into your bloodstream. Without regular exercise even the little pinpricks of everyday life can build up to poison your view of the world. Your bath will keep on insidiously filling. Over a period of time you will notice the symptoms of stress. Your mood will darken, or you will feel more intensely emotional about your problems. Some of the physical symptoms that accompany stress may occur. If you're prone to headaches, you'll notice the mild headaches starting again, or if you're an insomniac when you're stressed, you'll have the odd sleepless night. At worst you could have angry outbursts, or take to your bed with depression; at best you'll feel life is getting out of control.

If you have addressed your problems and taken the action you need to and switched off, this will not happen nearly as rapidly, but over a period of time your stress will inevitably increase to the point where you're not managing as well as you could. If you don't exercise, no matter what you do to control your stress, your thinking will be less clear, your memory will be worse, your mood will be lower, and you are more likely to suffer the physical symptoms of stress.

Even if you carry out the other stress management steps, you will still need to exercise.

What sort of exercise?

Only aerobic exercise is sufficient to reduce your stress levels. The word aerobic probably has bad press in the eyes of many who don't exercise. It conjures up images of leotards and grim faces, sweating bodies dancing to music and classes with the instructor exhorting you to 'Burn, burn, feel the pain!' But the term aerobic literally means with air. Aerobic exercise is exercise that increases your heart rate sufficiently for the heart and the lungs to transport oxygen to the working muscles during exercise. Only aerobic exercise gets the blood re-circulating into the extremities of your body rather than remaining in the central part of your body. Only aerobic exercise gets your endorphins going. The greater your aerobic fitness, the longer you're able to carry on any physical activity – whether it's running, riding a bike, swimming or playing sports – without suffering undue physical strain.

You don't have to be a top flight athlete in order to be fit aerobically and to reduce your stress, and as you will see shortly, there may be some reasons why you might not want to strive to be the best in your field. Being this desperate for fitness may have a counterproductive effect on your stress level.

> *Only aerobic exercise is sufficient to reduce your stress levels. It increases your heart rate sufficiently for the heart and lungs to transport oxygen to the working muscles.*

Ways to increase aerobic fitness

If you're not going to run a marathon or play top flight squash, what is the best way to increase your aerobic fitness? Activities that get you aerobically fit are basically those of an endurance nature which involve large muscle groups. These activities include:

- jogging
- running
- swimming
- aerobics
- circuit training
- cycling
- brisk walking – walking leisurely won't do it because it doesn't increase your heart rate.

Some sports will also fulfil the requirements of aerobic exercise; but many sports will not make you aerobically fit on their own, unless you've trained beforehand, because of their start-stop nature: the periods of intense activity are generally interspersed with periods of standing about doing nothing. Soccer, for example, or basketball, or even tennis and squash, can be like this.

If you're planning to play very vigorous sports like tennis and squash, you should achieve a basic level of fitness first before tackling them, because the intensity of these sports and people's competitive natures may result in sports injuries for the novice exerciser.

You may think that weight lifting would be good exercise; certainly it will build your muscles, but weight lifting is basically an anaerobic exercise – it doesn't increase your heart rate enough to reliably cut your stress level. Having said that, though, research into the relationship between exercise and endorphin production has shown that under some conditions weight lifting is aerobic and will release beta-endorphins. The critical factors are the number of repetitions and the interval between sets. If you use a weight light enough to allow 10 or 12 repetitions at a time and wait only a minute between sets, your heart rate remains high and your beta-endorphins will increase. If you use a weight so heavy you can only lift it five or six times and rest between sets for three minutes, your heart rate drops and your endorphin levels do not rise.

Circuit training

Aerobic circuit training with weights is one of the best activities for reducing your stress. In circuit training you move fast; you're working against time and you exercise many different parts of your body. You go from one set of weights to another without a pause, and it's the pauses that allow your heart rate to drop back down again; it's the same effect that you get if you rest for three minutes between sets when you're lifting weights.

Studies with older people have shown that for people in their seventies and eighties, circuit training is actually more effective than any other form of exercise in producing a positive mental attitude to life and reducing osteoporosis, the increase in porosity and brittleness of bones that occurs during old age.

Exercising your heart

An additional benefit of aerobic exercise is not only that the stress chemicals no longer affect you, but also that your heart muscle becomes stronger. Aerobic exercise exercises your heart. You would think that your heart gets enough exercise pumping 24 hours a day, seven days a week as it does, but because it's a muscle, when you're stressed, it also becomes tense and constricted, like every other in your body. The heart is the most important muscle in your body and so it needs to be exercised more regularly than any other.

*Another benefit of aerobic exercise is that your
heart muscle becomes stronger.*

How to choose your exercise

If you want to enjoy your exercise and stick to your program, look first at the
reasons why people exercise on pages 170–172. Check out which of these are
important to you. Socialising? A sense of challenge? Competition? Make sure
that the exercise you choose provides these for you. The following are some
more practical pointers.

Avoiding injury

You should be selective about the form of exercise you do, in order to avoid
injury. Many of the hard contact sports, football and the like, can be quite
dangerous, but even running or jogging can be harmful if you don't run
correctly. It's important to have the right shoes and to check that your running
style does not put undue strain on your body. Runners are more likely to need
hip replacement operations as they get old than non-runners, and woman
runners suffer more from prolapsed uteruses than women who do not run.

When you decide what kind of exercise you are going to do, you need to
look at both your age and your existing level of fitness. If you are over 30 or if
you haven't exercised regularly for a long time, you would be wise to speak to
your doctor first before you start your program. Once you have been given a
medical clearance it might be a good idea to have a program designed for you
by a qualified professional, someone with training in both exercise and health.
This way you can get something that is tailored to your age, to your fitness and
to your lifestyle, and a plan that will also take into account any existing injuries
or ailments you may have, such as a bad back or arthritis.

If you can't afford to do this, swimming is generally considered to be a safe
and effective form of aerobic exercise because the water supports your body.
Swimming exercises your whole body without placing undue strain on any one
area. Aqua-aerobics and water walking also have the same effect.

Power walking

Many people, particularly older people, swear by power walking or fast
walking. Power walking seems to be sweeping the world. It doesn't put the

same strain on the body as running. Most communities now have some form of power walking club. These operate throughout the day as well as in the early mornings, and sometimes in the evenings, for people who work during the day.

The gym

You may want to choose the convenience of the gym or the fitness centre for your exercise. There you can have an exercise program especially tailored to your needs. But a word of caution: if you are very unfit, overweight or disabled in some way, it's wise to make sure that the person who designs your program is qualified to take these elements into account.

If you choose to exercise by going to a gym, do a comparison shop first. Most gyms will allow you to pay a one-time fee to try out the facility before you join. Test out the equipment first. It may be in bad repair or there may be so many members that you have to wait ages to use each piece of equipment. If you have to wait around a lot at the gym, you won't be able to maintain aerobic activity, your heart rate will drop and your exercise will be less effective at reducing stress. When you're checking out a gym, make sure you go there at the time you will be going when you start your regular program, then you will be able to see just how busy it is.

How hard to exercise?

Warm-up

It's generally accepted that you should include a warm-up activity prior to strenuous exercise, and a cool-down after you exercise. If you allow your body to prepare itself by warming up first, you'll have fewer pulled muscles and other physical problems. Most gyms will design you an exercise program which includes warm-ups and cool-downs. A warm-up generally consists of light walking or a period on the exercycle to get the blood flowing in your legs, followed by some light stretching and callisthenics.

> *You should include a warm-up activity prior to strenuous exercise and a cool-down afterwards.*

Exercise

The exercise itself needs to be hard enough to make you perspire and to ensure that your heart rate is increased to between 60 to 80 percent of your maximum rate possible. You can easily figure out what your maximum rate is, in beats per minute, by subtracting your age from 220. For example, if you're 20 years of age, then 220 minus 20 = 200 beats a minute. You should not exercise at this level, it's too high, but if you want to be sure that you're exercising hard enough to cut your stress level, that is, exercising aerobically, you should try to raise your heart rate to between 60 percent and 80 percent of whatever your maximum heart rate is. If you're aged 20, it's 200 beats per minute, and that means exercising with your heart beating between 120 and 160 beats per minute.

> *The exercise needs to be hard enough to make you perspire and to ensure that your heart rate is increased to 60–80 percent of your maximum rate possible.*

Check your heart rate while you're exercising to see whether it's at the level you want. Exercise, then count your pulse for 10 seconds, and multiply it by six. If your heart rate is between 120 and 160, the intensity of your exercise is acceptable for a 20-year-old, but if it is above 160, then the exercise is probably too vigorous for you and you need to cut it back. If your heart rate is below 120, then you can probably increase the intensity. Obviously, if you are older than 20, you will reach your 80 percent and 60 percent limits at a lower number of beats per minute.

If you can't take the time to count your heart rate, then a good rule of thumb is to look at whether you can talk while you exercise.

> *If you can't talk comfortably while you're exercising, then you're probably pushing things too hard.*

Cool down

Taking time to cool down after your exercise is also very important. If you make sure that you walk around and stretch your leg muscles after you have finished exercising, you won't get blood pooling in the extremities. It is this that makes you aching and stiff later.

How long to exercise?

There's much more consensus on how long you need to exercise than there is on how often. It's generally accepted that between 30 and 40 minutes of exercise is enough both to get you fit and to cut your stress levels.

Recent research has looked more closely at the effects of different durations of exercise on reducing blood pressure. The researchers in one study wanted to see whether 10 minutes of exercise was as good as 40 minutes. People with normal or high blood pressure attended the local medical school and were asked to pedal an exercycle there on four consecutive days for either 10 or 40 minutes. Their blood pressure was measured before the study started and again on the fifth day, to see what changes there had been.

Ten days later all participants in the study were asked to return to the medical school for another four days. The group who had exercised for 10 minutes a day were now asked to exercise for 40 minutes, while those who had exercised for 40 minutes were asked to exercise for 10 minutes a day.

> *Between 30 and 40 minutes of exercise is enough*
> *both to get you fit and to cut your stress levels.*

The design of the study was quite sophisticated because each person was used as their own control group, that is, the study controls for the effects of individual differences in blood pressure levels and the amount these might vary in different people. It also allowed the researchers to find out whether people with high blood pressure would react in the same way as those with normal blood pressure.

The results of the study showed that 40 minutes of aerobic exercise lowered all participants' blood pressure, but that 10 minutes did not. That is, 40 minutes of exercise will reduce your stress level where 10 minutes won't.

However, some other studies suggest that you don't necessarily need to do the 30 or 40 minutes exercise all at one time. Researchers in the United States, at the Stanford University School of Medicine, looked at the effect of moderate exercise spread throughout the day in short bursts and compared it with longer periods of exercise on the same number of days a week.

Participants in this study were engineers who, at the time the study started, were not involved in regular exercise. Half of them were told to walk briskly or jog at a moderate pace for 30 minutes, five times a week. The other half were required to walk briskly or jog at a moderate pace but only for 10 minutes at a time, three times a day, five days a week. The amount of exercise in the two groups was identical, the difference lay in whether it was spread throughout the day or done all at once. The study continued for eight weeks.

After eight weeks everyone was assessed in terms of their levels of fitness, their blood pressure and their weight loss. All the men had obtained essentially the same level of fitness or cardio-vascular efficiency, the same drop in blood pressure levels and the same weight loss, regardless of whether they had exercised for 10 minutes at a time or for 30. Researchers concluded that the exercise just had to be regular and that even short spurts of activity can stimulate your metabolism, improve your oxygen uptake and decrease your blood pressure.

> *You don't need to do the 30 or 40 minutes all at one time.*

How often to exercise?

It's generally accepted that the minimum number of times you need to exercise is three times per week and that every second day is better. But most studies which look at the benefits of exercise examine its effect on fitness, rather than on stress. There is some suggestion from research into stress that exercising more frequently than three times per week may be better for dealing with your stress.

> *You need to exercise at least three times per week;*
> *more frequently may be better for dealing with stress.*

High blood pressure is a frequent symptom of stress. Research on the relationship between exercise and blood pressure has found that 40 minutes of brisk walking three times a week is sufficient to lower your blood pressure, but that daily exercise is better than three times a week for keeping it under control. If you're well attuned to your own individual physical symptoms of stress, and if you exercise regularly and reasonably frequently, you can probably figure out for yourself when your stress level is building up.

Monitor your stress symptoms

Even the research that is done on stress and how often you need to exercise doesn't generally look at the effects of exercise on your overall level of stress. It is more likely to look at one particular symptom of stress such as blood pressure. If you want to know how often you personally need to exercise, you're probably best to take every second day as the minimum and to monitor your own stress symptoms now that you know them. Monitor your own state of mind too – your tendency to think defeatist, paranoid or negative thoughts – to see whether you need to exercise daily. If you find that your thoughts are becoming negative when you skip a day's exercise even though your physical symptoms aren't extreme you'll probably benefit from daily exercise. Do check out first that you're also doing the other four stress management steps because you cannot expect exercise to control your stress if you're not doing these as well.

I know when I need to exercise now, my body tells me. My worst symptom of stress is insomnia; that's where it hits me most. I'm fine if I exercise every two or three days, but if I don't exercise for four days I really know it. I'll wake up in the middle of the night. I'll be in a cold sweat, and my head is full of deadlines and things undone. The world seems a scary place and I'm a victim within it, and I'll start thinking that I no longer believe in my ability to do anything. I feel like a huge tidal wave of work is about to overwhelm me.

If I've gone to the gym within the last couple of days I don't even wake up in the middle of the night, or if by chance I do, and the unfinished business starts coming back to me, I just think to myself, 'Oh well, it will get done, it always does; I'd rather be busy than idle.' And I turn over, and I go back to sleep again.

When to exercise?

People often ask whether it's better to exercise in the morning or in the evening. It probably depends upon when you can fit it into your schedule and when you have most need for it. Look at your stress diary to see when your greatest periods of stress are. If they are mostly in the day, at work, for example, you're better to exercise before you go to work. Then your head will be clear, the endorphins will be flowing and you will be able to tackle your work problems in a constructive way.

> *I'm writing my Master's thesis at the moment, and before I sit down to the keyboard, I will always go for a run, because I know that when I get back I'll be doing my best work, I'll be creative and more rational than if I just get straight out of bed and sit down to write. Exercise is great before an exam too. I've been in exams where I didn't feel confident, because I wasn't sure whether I had done enough study, and I've had total mental blank outs and done far worse than I needed to. But if you exercise beforehand, your memory is fantastic, your thinking is clear and you're able to integrate all the facts you do know, to pull everything together for a good answer.*

On the other hand, if it seems that your day is fine but most of your stress occurs in the evenings, when you come home to the family or when you're at home and lonely on your own, then exercise in the evenings.

If sleeplessness is one of your stress symptoms, exercising later in the day will probably result in a better night's sleep, provided you don't wind yourself up again with upsetting thoughts before you get into bed. Not only will it remove the stress chemicals that arouse you during the night but it increases your body's production of serotonin, a chemical involved in sleep. But if you exercise too late in the day, you may find that you're still too alert to sleep well at your normal bedtime.

If you've got a particularly stressful situation coming up, you'll always get through it far better if you exercise beforehand than if you don't.

> *When you exercise depends upon when you can fit it into your schedule and when you have most need for it.*

I can't force myself to do it

Many people hate exercise and seize any excuse or opportunity not to do it. If you are one of them, you'll know you want to exercise because you want the ultimate benefits: you want to be clear and calm and happy, and fit and healthy and in control of your life, but dragging yourself out there relentlessly day after day is just too much. How can you stick to your program? How can you make sure that you do that essential 30 or 40 minutes, week after week?

There has been a good deal of research on exercise compliance, on what it is that makes people stick with their exercise programs and on what distinguishes those who exercise regularly from those who don't.

First of all, you're more likely to stick to your program if you've selected a form of exercise that gives you most of what motivates you and is within your capabilities. So choose your exercise carefully if you want to be sure you'll stay with it. Check back to the section on page 176: 'How to Choose Your Exercise'.

> *You're more likely to stick to your program if you enjoy the type of exercise and it is within your capabilities.*

What makes people give up on exercise? Research in sports medicine suggests that the most common excuses for not exercising are: 'I don't have the time ... I'm too tired to be bothered ... There's nowhere I can go to exercise ... I don't know what exercise I should be doing, and ... I don't have any willpower'.

'I don't have time'

It is recommended that you exercise at least every second day. What if you think you don't have time to exercise that often? Well, you need to take heed of the Earl of Derby's statement at the beginning of this chapter.

You are more likely to become ill if you don't exercise, whether you're stressed or not. But don't despair about a lack of time to exercise, because exercise actually makes time. If you exercise regularly, you will find that not only is your mental state more positive, but also you get through far more in the course of your day. Everything that you do will be done more rapidly, all your decisions will be made with greater clarity, your planning will be better, your problem-solving will be more creative and your ideas will flow more freely.

Not having time is really a matter of priorities; people do what they enjoy. If you don't, you won't make the time to do it; but no matter how busy you are, you probably will do other things you enjoy, like watch television, read a newspaper or go to a movie.

> *Having time is a matter of priorities and doing what you enjoy.*
> *Exercise actually makes time by giving you more energy*
> *for your daily tasks.*

'I'm too tired'

Being too tired is usually a matter of mental, rather than physical, fatigue. If you've had a day full of stress, you won't feel like facing another chore at the end of the day. So it's important that your exercise is enjoyable. Even if you are physically fatigued as well as mentally, exercise dramatically increases your energy levels. Herbert Vries, an expert in ageing at the University of South California, has shown that men and women of 60 or 70 who start exercising regularly can become as fit and energetic as 30- or 40-year-olds who don't exercise. When he questioned his subjects about what they saw as the greatest benefit of their exercise programs, they most often told him it was greater energy. The more often you exercise, the more energy you have.

I used to go to the gym after work. Sometimes it would be half past seven before I got there. I wouldn't have had any dinner and I'd be really tired and I'd be looking for any excuse not to go, but I would make myself go, because I knew that after about 20 to 30 minutes I would feel the endorphins start. I knew that I would be looking at the world in a different way, that I wouldn't be tired and I wouldn't be feeling, 'How will I get through all the things I have to do?' I could also feel thoughts change from 'I've got too much to do' to 'I sure get through a lot'.

Try it out for yourself. Spend a week exercising and then a week not exercising. Monitor both your mood state and the amount of work that you achieve. Do it systematically; rate your state of mind on a 10 point scale, where 0 = feeling totally out of control of my life, and 10 = feeling totally in control of my life.

Rate, on a similar scale, the amount of your daily activities, where 0 = accomplished nothing, and 10 = accomplished all I planned.

Each evening give yourself a score on both your mood scale and your accomplishment scale. You'll be surprised at the difference during the week that you exercise; you will be happier, feel more in control and achieve more of your daily activities – provided of course, that you exercise in the way that is described here.

The more often you exercise, the more energy you have.

'There's nowhere I can go to exercise'

This is usually a cry of inconvenience rather than absence. Most towns have both public and private facilities for exercise and sports, but they may not always be sited where you want them to be. If they are not, you can still exercise without facilities – you can bike, jog or power walk. You can rent an exercise video, a stepper or an exercycle.

'I don't know what sort of exercise I should be doing'

This chapter will give you an understanding of what exercise does and how to go about selecting the exercise that's right for you. If you still have unanswered questions when you've finished the chapter, turn to an expert for advice.

'I don't have any willpower'

You may believe that willpower is something you're born with and if the good fairies didn't give you any at birth you'll never have it, but that is not true. Lack of willpower is really ignorance of the reasons why you're not able to stick to the task you've set yourself – whether it is exercise or any other task.

Read through this chapter again – especially the sections on what exercise does for you and this section on how to stick to your program – and see if you can diagnose your own problem. Are you telling yourself you're too tired, or that you don't have time to exercise? Are you a people person trying to exercise on your own?

Here are two tips you may find helpful in sticking to your exercise program, no matter what the causes of your difficulty.

1. Scheduling exercise into your day

You are much more likely to exercise if exercise is a regular part of your day than if you just try to fit it in somewhere. If you take the time for yourself and say, 'This is my time to exercise and I'm going to do it regularly and not allow anything else to get in my way', then exercise will become a part of the pattern of your day or become part of your routine. Anything that is a routine is likely to be carried out. You have all sorts of routines in your life that you perform without thinking, you just do them automatically, like cleaning your teeth or making your breakfast. They're not particularly pleasant in themselves but they get done because they tend to happen at the same time every day. If you have to knock out from your day something that you really like doing, in order to put in something that you don't like – exercise, for instance – you won't do it. Whereas if there's nothing else you planned or wanted to do in that time slot, you will exercise.

> *I find the only way I can really exercise regularly is to wake up at 5.30 in the morning. I set my alarm and I'm awake. I know I might as well get out and do it, because I have to get up in another hour anyway and there's no way that I'll be able to go back to sleep for that hour, especially when the sun's up and I can hear the birds.*

Another tip is to schedule your exercise before some activity you enjoy, before your dinner or before your favourite television program. This way you will be looking forward to something while you're exercising.

> *You are much more likely to exercise if exercise is a regular part of your day. Anything that is a routine is likely to be carried out. Schedule your exercise before some activity you enjoy.*

2. Cut the boredom factor

Many people who don't stick to their programs feel that exercise for its own sake can be very tedious. Exercising with a friend is probably more pleasant, because if you've got someone else to talk to while you're doing it, it takes your mind off the boredom. Having a personal trainer who sets progressive goals for you to achieve will also cut the boredom if you can afford it and it will also require you to schedule your exercise.

You can also reduce the boredom by doing something interesting while you're exercising. Read a book or magazine or watch television while you are riding your exercycle, or using your rowing machine or your stepper.

Additionally, you can make exercising on your own a lot less dull by using this time to think through problems, or for thinking creative thoughts, or for looking back on things that you have done well over the past few weeks. You will find that you get many of your best ideas while you're exercising.

> *Often if I've got a really difficult problem to work out or a hard choice to make, I'll save it until I'm exercising. I've done some of my most creative thinking*

sitting on the exercycle. This morning I decided on the layout for a big report I'm writing, I figured out how to put it to my boyfriend without upsetting him that I didn't want Christmas at his parents, and I planned a holiday for us in Fiji. These have all been on my mind for days. If I'm ever worried about something, I'll take it to the bike.

Your problems not only seem less but you can figure out better how to solve them. You can also use your exercise time to build your confidence. If you dwell on your strengths and your successes while you exercise you will find that you're clearer about what these really are, as well as being able to figure out how to improve on what you haven't done so well.

> *Cut boredom by exercising with a friend, having a personal trainer, doing something interesting while exercising, or using the time to think creatively.*

Cautions on exercise

Is exercise always good for reducing stress? There are two conditions under which it may not be. If you get too upset about not making progress with your program or not winning when you're playing sport, exercise may in fact produce more stress than it relieves. There are also some indications that if you exercise too much, this may be harmful to you.

It seems that you must have some feelings of success in the beginning of your exercise program, or your sporting activities, or you won't stick at them, you won't improve your skills and you will feel even more hopeless about your ability to control your life. It appears that the effects of exercise do depend on your view of it. If you've chosen an intensely competitive activity, or one that makes you feel so anxious you have to force yourself to do it, then your brain will release hormones and chemicals which produce stress rather than relieve it.

> *If you get too upset about not making progress with your*
> *program or not winning when you're playing sport,*
> *exercise may produce more stress than it relieves.*

If your view of your morning run with the club is that it's great to have some exercise and clear your head, and it looks like your time is improving a bit, then your body will release the endorphins and interferon that will make you feel positive and clear headed and strengthen your immune system. If your view of your morning run is that you have to do this exercise or you might get sick, and your times are falling off a lot lately and you really haven't got time to be doing this because you should be preparing for that difficult meeting coming up later in the day, then your body will be flooded with stress hormones and chemicals. Your immune response will be suppressed, your times will certainly be down, and you won't feel any better at the end of it than before you started.

People who feel like those in the latter category have been given the name the 'desperately well'. They are often people that we label type A personalities: perfectionists and achievers, cramming their lives with goals and activities. They feel guilty if they miss a single exercise session. According to wellness educator Mark Forgie, some of the desperately well have got to the stage where they can't feel well or in control of their lives if they have missed one exercise session or if they stop during exercise for 30 seconds and their heart rate falls.

> *You see them, people who desperately ski 12 hours a day, who then desperately*
> *spend time with their kids, who when they travel to Europe have to stay in a*
> *place that has a gym so they can desperately stick to their program. I mean*
> *who the hell goes to Vienna to do reps on a Stairmaster? It's crazy because*
> *there is just no peace in the whole thing.*

The largest and most comprehensive study done so far on the effects of exercise and health also found that some people didn't benefit as much from exercise as others. This is the Harvard University study that has been tracking the exercise patterns and health of Harvard graduates for over 50 years. Researchers in the Harvard study have found that regular exercise is an important factor in increasing length of life because it protects against heart disease. It also helps prevent colon cancer. Results showed that men who burnt

1000 calories (4180 kJ) a week in exercise had half the risk of colon cancer of men who took no exercise.

But the results of this study suggest that if moderate exercise is good, large amounts of exercise may not necessarily be better. Men in this study who played extremely strenuous sports and played them very often – sports like squash, and full court basketball – actually had higher death rates than men who exercised moderately. These men were burning more than 3500 calories (14,630 kJ) a week. Researchers concluded that you should probably not burn more than 3500 calories a week – this is equivalent to about six or eight hours of strenuous cycling or singles tennis. Even if you just walk 15 or more kilometres a week briskly so you burn off around 900 calories (3760 kJ), you can increase your life expectancy by 21 percent more than people who walk less than five kilometres a week. The evidence is clear: moderate exercise has definite benefits for your health.

> *Evidence shows that moderate exercise*
> *is better than large amounts.*

Other research has demonstrated that prolonged strenuous exercise can make you more susceptible to illness. Research on marathon runners showed that after three hours of very hard exercise, their blood displayed a 60 percent increase in cortisol, one of the stress hormones. Cortisol is one of the hormones that suppresses immune activity, which means that if you exercise in this way, you're actually more likely to come down with flu and viruses than if you don't. Similar effects on the immune system have been found in competitive swimmers, cyclists and skiers after very hard exercise.

Your Life Plan: Step 4

1. *Draw up an exercise plan for yourself.*
2. *Decide what exercise will suit you best, when you will do it and how often.*
3. *Think about how you will stick to your plan.*
4. *The following is a summary table of the points to remember when you are preparing a safe exercise plan:*

Fig. 8 Safe exercise plan

What sort of exercise?	Aerobic exercise: Power walking, swimming, aqua-aerobics, water walking, circuit training, jogging, running, rebounding, cycling, aerobic classes, exercise classes, skipping, rowing, rowing machines, stepping machines, treadmills, exercycles.
How hard should you exercise?	Work out your training heart rate in beats per minute: Subtract your age from 220 = your maximum heart rate (note: do not train at this rate) × by 0.6 = bottom training level; × by 0.8 = upper training level.
How long should you exercise?	30–40 minutes minimum.
How often should you exercise?	Every second day at least.
When should you exercise?	Analyse your stress diary – what time of the day do you need to reduce your stress most?
How will you stick to your exercise program?	Read carefully the section entitled: 'I can't force myself to do it' (pages 182–187). Schedule exercise into your day at a set time. Schedule exercise before something you enjoy doing. Exercise while doing something else: reading, watching television, solving problems, thinking about your strengths and successes.

Paul's Life Plan: Step 4

What sort of exercise?

I checked out the pump class at my local gym and decided it wasn't for me. I stood at the back of the class and watched a session. It all seemed a bit trendy and youthful, and I'm not a fan of the sort of music they play, although I did like the combination of strength work and an aerobic workout. So I got a training program organised and started on that. But after three or four weeks it started to fall by the wayside. I mean, I really wanted to do it, but I kept failing to get to the gym for one reason or another. I decided to work out why.

How to stick to my exercise

I thought about the squash I'd been playing. The good thing about it was that a court was booked for a certain time, which meant that you had to turn up. The downside was that if I didn't make it I felt bad, because I'd let my partner down. I realised that made me more likely to go. I decided that I did benefit by having a regular time set aside for exercise and so, for that reason, I did end up going to the pump class as well. It was every Tuesday and Thursday night at 7 and once I'd scheduled it in, I found it easy to turn up. I found I liked being one of a large number of people in a class. You felt you weren't alone and you could be as friendly or anonymous as you liked. And I amazed my 13-year-old son by being able to identify some of the music he buys.

Summing Up

Step 4: Keep fit and be happy
- Exercise reverses your stress cycle.
- Exercise releases chemical 'uppers'.
- Five other reasons you should exercise:
  1. Better health and fitness
  2. Improved appearance
  3. Enjoyment
  4. Social activity
  5. Psychological benefits
- Decide on the best exercise program.

Prevent stress and change your chemistry

Step 5: Do the things you enjoy

How sour sweet music is,
When time is broke and no proportion kept,
So it is in the music of men's lives.

WILLIAM SHAKESPEARE

Why enjoyment is important

If you have been following the steps in this book one by one, you can regard this chapter as the final part of a round-the-world yacht race. By now you are no longer fighting raging storms and mountainous seas; broken masts and waves as big as buildings are all behind you. You are sailing calmly into port to the worldwide congratulations, champagne, caviar, good friends, fun and laughter.

Once you have read this chapter through, you should put all the steps, including Step 5, into action at once. You will be more effective at managing your tension if you do, because taking control of your life is not just about stemming the flow of stress; it's also about doing things that will prevent it and that will enhance your life. It is without doubt that stress and unhappiness are caused by both the presence of things negative and the absence of things positive.

> *Taking full control of your life is about creating a life that is balanced by events and activities that will fill you with the positive emotions: like joy and satisfaction and a sense of achievement.*

Pay as much attention to what is written here as you have to the contents of the previous eight chapters. It is as important.

If you are contented and at peace with yourself, many other benefits will accrue to you. The effects you have on others around you, for example, will be quite different than if you are depressed, bitter or angry.

You can probably manage your stress well enough if you do only Steps 1 through 4. But unless you do Step 5 as well, it will be a struggle. Step 5 is the difference between surviving and living.

> *It is not true that suffering ennobles the character; happiness does that sometimes, but suffering for the most part makes men petty and vindictive.*
>
> W. SOMERSET MAUGHAM

Balance

For your body to function optimally it needs to be in a state of balance, or equilibrium. This is known as allostasis, in which all your organs and systems operate as they should regardless of the circumstances you are experiencing, whether you are sleeping, exercising or engaged in some other activity. If your body is temporarily out of kilter, as it is when it is under stress or when you are sick, it needs to be able to return to this state of allostasis. It is the role of the parasympathetic nervous system to restore this equilibrium after you have become stressed, but as Chapter 1 outlines, it is not always able to do this. If your body cannot maintain allostasis, you become seriously ill, or some organ will break down and your body ceases to work as it should.

> *If your body is out of balance biochemically, it is important that you remedy this if you can.*

You read in Chapters 1 and 2 about what happens when the delicate balance of your hormonal activity is disrupted either by too much stress or by illness or ageing. When your biorhythms become unregulated, your emotions are changed and you become more easily stressed or depressed. One of the culprits that makes you more easily stressed is low levels of thyroid hormones.

Thyroid imbalance

If you feel your ability to cope with stress is getting less as the years go by, even though the causes of your stress have not increased, see your doctor for a check on your thyroid hormone levels. If these levels are low or borderline you may want to have a series of tests at three monthly intervals. If your levels are dropping over the series that's usually a good indication that your difficulties coping with stress may have a thyroid component. Fortunately, thyroid hormone levels can be stabilised quite easily with replacement thyroid hormones.

In my forties I was fit and strong, and I had boundless energy. I was also enthusiastic, motivated and confident about making changes in my life. I trained for and started a completely new career, moved to a new country, made new friends, and set up my own business. Nothing worried me. My fifties were different. I continued in my job but the whole thing bored me, and I didn't have the confidence any longer to start something new. Little things began to get on top of me. I stopped seeing my friends as often. I didn't always feel like calling them. I got through the day all right, but by the time I dragged myself home in the evening, I was exhausted and just wanted to sit down with a meal and the TV. The thought of picking up the phone and talking to anyone was exhausting. I didn't answer the phone if it rang. Of course, people stopped ringing. Then I started to get paranoid and thought that nobody liked me anymore and I got paranoid about the way I looked too. No matter what I did, I couldn't lose any weight. Gradually, I got fatter and fatter. I decided that this must be what getting old is all about. Then, luckily I went to have some blood tests for an insurance policy and my doctor got them to test my thyroid levels. They were borderline, so she prescribed me some Thyroxine for a month to see if it made any difference. The first day I took it, I caught myself running down the hall. I thought, 'I haven't done that for as long as I can remember. I didn't have that 4 p.m. feeling of exhaustion, and I came home and spent the evening on the phone inviting all the people I hadn't seen in months to a party. I now feel as I did in my thirties.

> Diminishing ability to cope with stress may be due to low or borderline thyroid hormone levels.

Sex hormone imbalance

Another biochemical loading for increased stress or depression is an imbalance or deficiency in your sex hormones – estrogen, progesterone and testosterone. Because some of the symptoms of a sex hormone deficiency may be identical to those of an excess, you won't always be able to tell which of your hormones are out of balance. For this reason, if you are within the vulnerable age group and you suspect that your anger, anxiety, depression, fatigue or difficulty concentrating and remembering may be hormonally related, or if you suffer from any of the hormone-related disorders listed on page 57, ask your doctor to test your estrogen, progesterone and testosterone levels. As with a thyroid decline, the most telling indicator that the hormonal changes of ageing are affecting your happiness is the feeling that your ability to cope with stress is worse as the years go by, even though the causes of your stress have not changed. It is important to note here that a recent study which found detrimental effects on women of hormone replacement therapy looked at women who were using synthetic hormones, that is, not those molecularly equivalent to what your body produces, and that these women were all given the same dosage. You do need to replace only what your body has lost.

> An imbalance or deficiency in your sex hormones – estrogen, progesterone and testosterone – can cause stress and depression.

To eliminate your hormonal symptoms you must achieve a hormonal balance. There is now good evidence that estrogen alone can be rapidly effective in treating depression in women who are pre-menopausal or menopausal. But more compelling perhaps is research which shows that giving older women estrogen plus androgens (progesterone and testosterone are androgens), that is, replacing all the hormones lost as you age, leads to a greater improvement in depressive symptoms, as well as in fatigue, lack of concentration, decreased libido and inability to achieve orgasm, than giving estrogen alone. There is also good evidence that replacing testosterone combats depression in older men whose testosterone levels have dropped. Balance is important, however. Research shows that, while increases of testosterone reduce your depression if you have low levels of the hormone, increases may cause depression if you have average or high levels to start with. Of course, not everyone views the effects of hormonal decline negatively.

> *At last I am free of that savage and fierce master.*
>
> SOPHOCLES

A balanced life

Depression is also likely when your life is unbalanced. You can withstand an enormous amount of stress if at the same time you do things that bring you happiness, joy and hope. Research is just starting to support the observations of clinicians and psychologists that the difference between people who manage their stress and people who don't, and who then become depressed, is that the former are still involved in activities that they enjoy.

> *You can withstand an enormous amount of stress if at the same time you do things that bring you happiness, joy and hope.*

Enjoyment balances out stress

The way enjoyment insulates you against stress and depression makes sense if you remember the research on loss of control, learned helplessness and depression. In the Introduction you learned that some researchers believe that a loss of control over your life causes you to become helpless, which in turn makes you depressed. If you have activities in your life that you enjoy, you are in control of these. Not all of your life is out of your grasp.

But it is not quite as straightforward as simply having that balance in your life; you need to make sure you keep it there. Stress is insidious because it can steal away your enjoyment in life. When you're under pressure for a long time, you may feel you don't get the same enjoyment from anything as you used to. Everything becomes an effort and you know you're starting to burn out.

It is possible to see a mechanism for both of these phenomena: the insulating effect of enjoyable activities against depression and the loss of pleasure in them when you're under stress for a long period. Remember that you can only hold one thought in your head at a time. If part of your day is spent thinking about things that make you feel good, you have turned off the stress cycle for that period. Positive thoughts act as alleviators of stress.

One of the few researchers who have studied positive emotions such as joy and contentment, Barbara Frederickson of the University of Michigan, has focused on how positive emotions such as joy, contentment and love help to build your character and personal resources. She theorises that positive emotions have an evolutionary significance. Unlike negative emotions, which narrow people's thoughts and actions, positive emotions broaden their thoughts and their actions. She says joy creates the urge to play, interest fosters the urge to explore, and contentment spurs the desire to savour and integrate. Frederickson maintains that positive emotions build your ability to discover new actions, ideas and social bonds, which in turn will build your physical, intellectual and social resources. She believes that you can transform yourself through experiencing positive emotions to become more creative, resilient, socially integrated and healthy.

> *If stress is always around, you must balance it with activities and events that will provide you with emotions that are positive.*

Unfortunately, what often happens when you're under stress is that you feel so exhausted that you can end up cutting out of your life everything that makes you happy. Your body becomes extremely tired when you're stressed, because your organs are working twice as hard as they should. You have no energy and you feel unmotivated. You use what little energy you have to deal with the essentials, and they're usually the stressful issues. You can't be bothered doing the things you used to enjoy. You'd rather vege out in front of television instead of going out with friends; you'd rather stay at home than go to night school and take the navigation course which will allow you to go sailing next summer. And so you systematically eliminate from your life all the things that you used to enjoy, everything that used to balance your life, everything that took your mind off your problems. You're then left with nothing positive in your life, nothing to look forward to any longer, no hope, just the black thoughts, distressing emotions and physical anguish of stress. That, generally, is when depression takes you over.

If you have a life in which stress is always lurking – as many of us do – you must balance it with activities and events that will provide you with emotions that are positive, and you must keep it balanced.

However, positive thoughts don't just take your mind off the things that stress you. The complete explanation for why you'll manage your stress 100 percent better if you do things you enjoy is much more complex – and much more interesting.

Mood altering chemicals

Your brain is awash in a sea of chemicals that affect your thinking and your emotions. One estimate is that only 29 of the thousands of neurotransmitters your brain produces have been identified and tracked. Dr Florian Holsboer, of the Max Planck Institute in Munich, divides these chemicals into an orchestra of three sections. Those known as opiates produce a dreamy, numbing effect. The second group, under the direction of corticotrophin-releasing hormone, produce an anxiety reducing and sleep inducing effect similar to benzodiazepines. The third group: serotonin, the neuroamines and the endorphins, produce energy and arousal. According to Lionel Tiger, world famous anthropologist, 'Hope is associated with a secretion just as despair is. In general, people successful at operating their lives must have the capacity to generate this neuro-bath themselves.'

Researchers have now found that exciting activities cause your brain to release neurotransmitters such as dopamine. Dopamine, one of the third group of chemicals, gives you pleasure and increases your arousal level. Even more recent research has found that merely thinking positively also alters your brain's biochemistry. We don't know yet which of the chemicals in the orchestra it releases, but we do know it makes you feel good and it helps you combat stress.

The group of mood altering substances most researched so far are endorphins. You will remember endorphins were mentioned in Chapter 8, the chapter on exercise. They are from the third group, chemicals that make you feel confident, energetic and optimistic.

The field of endorphin research and of research into other chemicals that alter your moods is, while not exactly in its infancy, certainly not in its prime. A lot of the results are still confusing. However, there are some facts that are clear.

Low endorphins: bad moods

Your body has a certain base level of endorphins circulating constantly in your bloodstream that influences your moods. At certain periods of your day and your year, and at certain periods of your life, they may be higher or lower. When they are low, your mood is down, making you more vulnerable to stress. For example, some studies have found that endorphin levels are low in women in the pre-menstrual period. Women who report the PMT blues or even the PMT rages will identify with this effect on their emotions. It appears that the low progesterone of PMT somehow causes low endorphin levels. However, it is likely that all the sex hormones affect your endorphin levels. During menopause all three sex hormones – estrogen, progesterone and testosterone – decrease.

Menopause

For many years women who complained that they were depressed during menopause were laughed at or were told they were suffering mid-life crisis or empty nest syndrome, but research suggests that they were right after all. Post-menopausal women have lower circulating beta-endorphin levels than fertile women. When menopause has not been natural but has been surgically brought about, through a hysterectomy, for instance, as much as a 40 percent decrease in circulating endorphin levels has been observed.

Hormone replacement therapy, after either normal or surgically induced menopause, is followed by a significant increase in circulating beta-endorphins. Women who have been depressed during menopause and have undergone hormone replacement therapy will frequently report changes in their mood, an increase in optimism and a belief that they can go on with their lives.

Pregnancy

Pregnancy is also a condition in which changes in endorphin levels occur. Towards the end of pregnancy and during labour there is an increase in the mother's endorphin levels. The maximum increase occurs during the birth. Since endorphins are painkillers as well as mood elevators, it makes sense that during birth, which is for many women the most agonising experience of their lives, the body would naturally provide some counterbalance to the pain. Endorphins may also have a role to play in postnatal depression. Levels of beta-endorphins between the first and the fifth day after a baby is born are significantly lower than they are before the baby is born.

Childhood

Even in children, there is a discernible daily fluctuation of beta-endorphin levels. All parents are familiar with 'hell-time', five to seven in the evening, when children tend to be hyperactive, moody and emotional. Researchers tested a group of six-year-olds and found that a definite circadian rhythm exists in children of that age, with low values of beta-endorphins in the evening hours. Parents usually attribute 'hell-time' to hunger, but it is obviously not only hunger that makes your children cranky and irritable around dinner time.

Depression and endorphins

Do we know anything about the effects of very low levels of endorphins? A post-mortem study on the brains of people who committed suicide showed that they had very low levels of beta-endorphins and of serotonin compared with people who died in traffic accidents. The researchers decided that the mechanisms that produce endorphins may not function properly in people who are driven to suicide. Other studies have compared the endorphin levels of underweight anorexic patients with the endorphin levels of healthy, normal-weight women. Anorexia is correlated with mood changes, depression and hopelessness. Anorexic patients were found to have significantly lower endorphin levels than their healthy, normal-weight counterparts.

Diseases such as Alzheimer's disease are also associated with depression or anxiety or anger. Families consistently report that members who develop this disorder suffer enormous changes in personality. Sweet, gentle and inoffensive parents can become raging tyrants. Several groups of researchers have found a reduced concentration of beta-endorphins in patients with Alzheimer's disease, which could partly explain these changes in mood.

High endorphins: joy, optimism and no pain

At the other end of the scale, when the levels of endorphins in your bloodstream are high, you can be aware of the change in your mood in the other direction. We talked about the way exercise produces 'runner's high'; feelings you experience when you have a high level of endorphins in your bloodstream can range from joy and euphoria through optimism to calmness and confidence.

Paradoxically, another trigger that releases endorphins into your bloodstream is stress. You might ask why you don't feel their effects when you are stressed. You do feel them, but not as an emotional high. The depressant effects of your stress chemicals are too strong for the endorphins to alter your mood, but you do feel their effect as painkillers rather than mood elevators.

Mothers running through burning houses to rescue their children say they didn't feel the fire; people battling intruders in their homes don't know they're hurt until afterwards; victims of domestic violence, both children and women, will tell you they get to a stage where the beatings no longer hurt. In all these cases the fear you experience is so extreme that the amount of endorphins released has blocked your perception of pain.

Our universal 'uppers'

What are the activities you should put into your life to balance and to enhance it? Are they solely dependent on your individual preferences? Or are there some things that are universally able to make you feel less stressed? Some things are idiosyncratic – they are your individual preferences and you may enjoy them but your neighbour may not. Some sources of enjoyment, though, are common to every human being. They are the sources of enjoyment that are universal.

The following sections look at some of the activities that will help add balance to your life and enhance it.

Learn what will make you feel good

What makes you happy?

> *Live not as though there were a thousand years ahead of you,*
> *Fate is at your elbow,*
> *Make yourself good while life and power are still yours.*
>
> MARCUS AURELIUS

What do you think is going to make you happy? If you look at the advertising that is all around you – on television, on billboards, in the newspapers – you would think it was material possessions. But according to research, material possessions are not what make people happy, although they are what people think will make them happy. Only if you don't have enough money to put a roof over your head, food on the table and to keep yourself warm will money fully satisfy you.

In the United States surveys show that since the 1950s the buying power of Americans has doubled, but has the level of happiness doubled? Not at all. Michael Argyle, British researcher in happiness, reports that while achieving a high status profession may make you happy, money is much less important. There hasn't been a great deal of research into happiness, but for centuries writers and philosophers have suggested that the active pursuit of happiness is an illusion, that it is not by trying to be happy that you will become so but by living in accordance with your values. Benjamin Spock once observed that happiness was mostly a by-product of what made people feel fulfilled.

One researcher in the area of happiness, American social psychologist David Myers, has a checklist of the things likely to bring you happiness. These are:

- Fit and healthy bodies
- Positive self-esteem
- Feelings of control
- Optimism
- An outgoing nature
- Acceptance and an outward focus
- Realistic goals and expectations
- Supportive friendships
- A close, intimate and equal relationship
- Challenging work
- Leisure pursuits – with adequate rest
- A faith that has purpose

You can see that the first seven of these are likely to be yours if you learn to manage your stress well. The last five are very similar to what researchers into human values have identified as universal priorities. For most people the important priorities in their lives are likely to be:

- Family
- Children
- Friends
- Financial security
- Leisure activities
- Sexual relationship
- Work or career
  (Not necessarily in that order.)

Living in accordance with your values will bring you contentment and satisfaction.

What are your values?

List now, in order of importance, the things in your life that you value. Use the two checklists here as a guide, but remember that they are only a guide, not a blueprint. You are an individual and there may be things more important to you than those listed here.

Do you live by your values?

Take a look at the life you live at the moment and compare it with your list. What are your priorities in life right now? Where do you spend most of your time, effort and energy? Are you living a life that is in accordance with your values? It's all too easy to become caught up in day-to-day coping, in dealing with the minutiae of life rather than in spending your time doing what is important to you. How many parents spend their lives working hard for the family instead of doing things with them? If you do this, you're in danger of waking up one day to find your children grown and gone and that the deep intimate relationship you could have had with them has never fully developed. On the other hand, how many people spend their time just living their lives, spending their money with never a thought for tomorrow? If you do that, you could wake up to find yourself 60 and penniless.

Set your goals

1. Look at your list of values and decide what changes you need to make so you will be living a life that is in accord with them. Set specific goals for yourself in each area. Start by sitting down and planning where you want to be in a year's time. Be specific. If you can't make these decisions alone, do it with a friend you trust.
2. Then work out what you need to reach your goals and what could prevent you from achieving them. If you can, do a time line for the intermediate steps. Remember that these plans are not set in stone; you can, and you should, alter them as your circumstances change.

Catalogue your pleasures

Besides the peace, contentment and satisfaction you'll feel from living in accordance with your values, activities that give you pleasure and enjoyment are important antidotes to stress. Of course, there is some overlap between these two – living in accordance with your values and doing things you enjoy. You'll undoubtedly derive enjoyment from getting close to your family, from doing well at your career or from finding some all-consuming passion that brings you bliss. But there are also many relatively minor ways in which you can increase your daily enjoyment of your life and prevent stress. If you put activities and events that give you pleasure into your life, you will naturally be thinking positive thoughts and feeling positive emotions like optimism, confidence, joy and hope, and you will win the battle more easily against your negative thoughts.

> *Activities that give you pleasure and enjoyment are important antidotes to stress.*

Look closely at your life. Do you have enough things in it that give you hope, fun, satisfaction, peace, joy, confidence, elation, adventure – all the pleasant emotions? Make a list of everything that makes you feel this way, large or small: a holiday overseas, a new house, a new car, or spending time with your children, a good book, an early night, sleeping late in the morning, breakfast in bed. You may not be able to afford all the large pleasures, but there will be many small ones that you may have dropped out of your life if you are stressed.

> *When I am feeling unhappy I put on some nice clothes and make-up and I drive the car. Controlling the car is associated with controlling my life. I go into the city and I'll go into the library and read and I go around art galleries and I'll go and have a good coffee and something nice to eat.*

Don't let money be a barrier. A walk in the sun or a day at the beach costs nothing, nor does a talk with a friend. Good friends are worth more than gold. C. S. Lewis once said that friendship was unnecessary, like philosophy and art, that it has no survival value; rather it is one of those things that give value to survival.

Plan pleasure in your life

Once you have catalogued all the activities you enjoy, sit down and plan how you will put them into your life. Schedule some into each day, and some into each week. Try to achieve a balance of activities you are obliged to do and activities you will enjoy doing, both daily and week by week. Put some of the enjoyments into the future too. The anticipation of an event is often better than the realisation of it.

> *Schedule some enjoyable activities into each day,*
> *and some into each week.*

Having things to look forward to gives you hope. Hope and desire are emotions essential to human wellbeing. When depression arrives, hope departs. When all hope is lost, the suicidal take the final step.

I went through a time in my life when everything went wrong: my marriage ended, I started a new job that was dreadfully difficult for me, I had no friends anymore, they don't want to know you when you're single. I got through it because I was determined to create my home as a place where I felt good: I filled it with flowers, I played the music I enjoyed, I cooked nice meals and ate them by candlelight, I read stimulating books and magazines and watched interesting videos, I lit fires in the winter, my bed was cosy and warm. I looked forward to coming home at the end of my day. Home was the only place I felt good.

Relax and recreate

Relaxation training is often used as a solution for the acute muscle tension experienced by many people who are stressed. Relaxation training has effects similar to meditation. It works by taking your mind off the negative thoughts that trigger off the stress reaction, and by physically relaxing muscles that have become tense through stress. But relaxation has a meaning broader than just relaxation training. The dictionary defines relaxation as: 'rest or refreshment, as after work or effort; recreation'. In physics the term relaxation means: 'the return of a system to equilibrium after a displacement from this state'. It is in this latter sense that relaxation is an essential part of combating your stress and balancing your life.

> *You need stress-free periods in order to return your system*
> *to its equilibrium.*

You need to have stress-free periods in your life – daily, weekly and yearly. These are times when you don't have to deal with any of the 'tough stuff', times when the pressure is off and your responsibilities are low. They may be occasions when you are actively doing things you enjoy, in the recreation sense of the word, or they may be times when you are just 'hanging out' doing nothing, taking a vacation, resting.

Get rest and sleep

Relaxation is a basic biological need. It returns your system to equilibrium. Recreation takes your mind off your troubles and stops the stress cycle. Rest, in particular sleep, allows your body to do a number of essential protective and restorative functions. If you are a normal, non-stressed, healthily functioning human being, a fair percentage of your day is spent in sleep. Your body simply cannot perform optimally without it. Sleep deprivation causes physical exhaustion and mental and emotional upset; it's probably a major contributor to depression. Studies in sleep laboratories in the United States show that subjects who are woken up frequently throughout the night become irritable and difficult and are unable to concentrate during the day.

Insufficient sleep also causes your immune system to break down. We have known for a long time that the three biggest killers of the immune system are poor diet, stress and insufficient sleep. More recently, science has discovered that having enough sleep has a beneficial effect on our immune system. Endorphins are present in your body all the time and their levels fluctuate both throughout the day and also over longer periods. Sleep releases these circulating endorphins into your bloodstream and they, in turn, boost your immune system. If you don't get enough sleep to meet your body's requirements, fewer endorphins will be released, and you're likely to feel lower in mood, more susceptible to pain and more vulnerable to illness.

> *You need to have adequate relaxation on a daily basis in the form of rest or sleep as well as longer periods of relaxation throughout your week.*

To have a balanced life and to feel that your life is under your control you need to have adequate relaxation on a daily basis in the form of rest or sleep. You also need to have periods of relaxation throughout your week as well. This is why you have weekends. If you can't create for yourself a balanced day during the working week, because, for instance, you have a job that requires long hours, then it is important that your weekend has some relaxation in it. Or, if you are in the sort of job which is more project oriented and doesn't run on a five working day cycle, you need to balance your periods of rest and recreation on a longer scale. If you have to work more than five days in a row, you should take off more than two days at the end of this. Don't skimp on your holidays either. Be aware of when you need them. Do you need three weeks at the end of the year, or will you feel better if you have a week three times a year?

Love and sex

Love looks not with the eyes but with the mind
and therefore is winged Cupid painted blind

WILLIAM SHAKESPEARE

Love also changes your biochemistry. Love is a natural high similar to being 'hyped up on cocaine' or 'speed'. The rush is fuelled by elevated levels of neurotransmitters: dopamine, norepinephrine, phenylethylamine and also testosterone and estrogen. Neurobiologists, sex researchers, anthropologists and other scientists are studying how chemical reactions lead you to romance and long-term relationships.

Sexual arousal and orgasm also cause your brain to release endorphins and another chemical, oxytocin. As well as improving your mood, sexual activity has been found to improve your breathing and circulation, your cardiovascular conditioning, and your flexibility and muscle tone. It has also been shown to relieve the symptoms of specific medical conditions such as menstrual problems, and osteoarthritis and to boost your immune system. Research has shown that people labelled as 'sex addicts' and others who move from affair to affair rather than face long term commitment may be deficient in oxytocin. These people discover that they cannot get the same 'sexual high' with the same person, so they move on to another conquest.

There is also experimental evidence which indicates that apart from exercise and sleep, there are four other things you can take charge of that will either release mood-elevating endorphins into your bloodstream or will elevate your mood chemically in some other way. These are:

* Food
* Massage

- Sunlight
- Laughter

If you're planning a balanced and positive life, you should take these four into account as well as all the other activities that alter your biochemistry. You can make sure they feature in your life regularly and you can use them to add to your background levels of endorphins or other chemicals at times when they are low, and get yourself emotionally 'over the hump' then. A life that's full of good food, regular massage, sunlight, fun and laughter doesn't sound too bad a life anyway.

Your diet and your moods

One cannot think well, love well, sleep well, If one has not dined well.
VIRGINIA WOOLF

Eat, drink and be merry

If your mother used to tell you to eat up all your breakfast because low blood sugar made you evil-tempered first thing in the morning, she may not have had the full picture. Probably low endorphin and low serotonin levels contributed more than a little to your irritability. Finishing everything on your plate raised these and made you nicer to be around. Research has shown that the intake of food is associated with an increase in blood levels of beta-endorphins, serotonin and other neurotransmitters. Several researchers have found that circulating levels of endorphins in obese subjects are higher than they are in normal-weight subjects. If food makes you feel good, perhaps the fat happy person is not such a myth after all. If you take refuge in the kitchen when you are stressed, it's not just to take your mind off your problems. There is a more basic biochemical reason why food makes you feel better. Neuroscientists now regard the potential of your diet to influence your brain chemistry and your behaviour as a fruitful avenue of investigation.

Man lives on one quarter of what he eats.
On the other three-quarters, his doctor lives.
5000-YEAR-OLD INSCRIPTION ON AN EGYPTIAN PYRAMID

Bad eating, bad moods, bad health

Eating well and sensibly is one of the basic disciplines for controlling stress and also for preventing it. It's quite common, when you're under pressure, for your eating to become disordered. You may eat less than normal. When the hydrochloric acid that secretes into your stomach during stress gives you feelings of nausea, or pains, you don't feel like eating. But if you don't eat, not only will you become physically weak, and less able to combat your stress, you will make the physical consequences of the acid secretion worse. At least if you have food in your stomach, the acid is not digesting the lining of your stomach. If it does, you'll end up with ulcers. Coating the lining of your stomach with an indigestible substance is one of the ways doctors prevent ulcers.

Eating well and sensibly is one of the basic disciplines for controlling and preventing stress.

When you're very depressed too, you often don't feel like eating. If your biorhythms are disordered, your brain ceases to get the normal messages to eat throughout the day, your body doesn't receive the nutrients it needs and your immune system starts to break down. By eating badly when your life is going wrong, your immune system receives a double blow: poor diet attacks your immune system, and so does stress. With your immune system already weakened by stress, eating poorly puts greater strain on it. You'll be even more likely to come down with flus, colds and viruses, and maybe something more serious. And you'll find it harder to get on top of your original stress: a bad diet doesn't help your moods – anorexics know that.

At the other end of the spectrum, you may find your eating is excessive when you're stressed. Overeating as a stress reaction is perhaps even more common than being unable to eat. But overeating won't make you less stressed; it's likely to increase your unhappiness. Problems with almost every body function occur more frequently if you are obese. But the repercussions from eating unwisely are not just physical; you will feel more tired and lethargic and usually more unconfident as well.

Tell me what you eat and I will tell you who you are.
ANTHELME BRILLAT-SAVARIN

If you're depressed or stressed, you're not only prone to alter the amount of food you eat, you're also likely to eat an unhealthy diet. When you feel your life is out of control you tend to skip meals, or to slip into erratic eating patterns and poor habits. High calorie junk food, fatty foods and sweet things seem more comforting when you're feeling down. But the comfort is illusory.

What is a good diet?

A healthy, varied and balanced diet is important for everyone, stressed or not. It is important to feed yourself well. After all, you are what you eat, and if you want to be fit and energetic and mentally alert to combat your stress and to make wise decisions about the things that need to be changed in your life, you need to give your body the nutrients that it requires.

There are as many ideas on healthy diets as there are pages in this book, but there are some accepted guidelines on what is good nutrition.

Eating a healthy diet is about food choice and a balanced food intake. You can incorporate all kinds of food and drink into your diet, because no food is bad for you. However, some foods should be eaten often and in abundance and some foods should be eaten in small amounts and only occasionally. This goes counter to many common assumptions. People believe that there are good and bad foods and that you should avoid the bad ones. What these beliefs do is lead people to be very selective about what they eat. This often means that you end up with a low intake of important nutrients. It is very important to eat a variety of foods. Balance is as important in what you eat as it is in every other area of your life.

> *It is very important to eat a variety of foods and have a balanced diet.*

Current research suggests that we may need less carbohydrate in our diet than was previously thought. But if your diet is too low in carbohydrate you won't feel vibrant and healthy. The role of carbohydrate is to provide energy for all your daily activities. Carbohydrates also produce serotonin, which raises your general sense of wellbeing. A high protein, low carbohydrate diet will lower your serotonin levels. But protein is important because it plays a crucial role in tissue repair, growth and maintenance. It also produces vital enzymes and hormones, and helps produce norepinephrine and dopamine, neurotransmitters that energise and keep you alert. A very low or no fat diet has implications for your ability to manage your stress too. A certain amount of fat is necessary to your body. Some vitamins are soluble only in fat and a lack of fat in your diet interferes with the body's absorption of these. Your body also needs a layer of fat to protect your internal organs and to keep you warm. In addition, all your sex hormones and some others are made from cholesterol. Fat is the best source of cholesterol. But excessive fat and cholesterol are likely to be the biggest health hazards for most people. Too much saturated fat and cholesterol is particularly implicated in coronary heart disease.

Other food components will also improve your mood. The omega 3 oils found in fish help prevent you getting depressed. Studies have shown that there is a 60-fold difference in depression rates between countries with the highest consumption of omega 3 oils, such as Japan and Taiwan, and countries with the lowest, such as North America, Europe and New Zealand. If you don't enjoy eating fish, omega 3 oils can also be found in walnuts, walnut oils, ground flax seed, and flax seed oils.

Omega 3 oils help prevent depression.

Deficiency in vitamin B6 and in vitamin B12 has also been associated with depression. Vitamin B12 deficiency is more likely if you are aged over 50. It is estimated that 10–30 percent of people over 50 can no longer assimilate the vitamin B12 in their food, but are not aware of this and suffer depression, memory problems, and even paranoia as a result. You can supplement your diet with moderate doses of vitamin B6 (three milligrams is recommended) and with supplements of vitamin B12. Supplements are preferred if you are vitamin B12 deficient because you can assimilate them even though you cannot process the foods that contain vitamin B12.

Zinc is another substance that may be related to your general sense of wellbeing. A study of 50- to 80-year-olds found that a third of these were deficient in zinc. Zinc deficiency has been implicated in pre-menstrual syndrome. It results in the decreased secretion of progesterone and opiates and endorphins. Zinc has many functions; it helps manufacture the body's proteins and genetic material. It is implicated in growth and taste perception, hormonal activity and immune function.

If you are planning to supplement your diet with these substances, remember the concept of allostasis. It is important that you don't supplement to excess, but that you allow your body to maintain its state of balance in your diet as in everything else.

Massage

We have known for a long time that the positive physical benefits of massage are reduction in pain and an increase in the circulation of blood and lymph in your body. Now researchers have found that you may get psychological changes attributable to massage. Certain types of massage release endorphins into your bloodstream and lower your levels of the stress hormone, cortisol. This results not only in a decrease in pain levels but also in stress levels. Massage is also used to help people with bulimia, an eating disorder characterised by cycles of starving and bingeing. It is believed that the low endorphin levels caused during the starve part of the cycle set up the craving for food, leading to the binge part of the cycle. Although massage doesn't cure bulimia, it has been found to control it, presumably by increasing the low endorphin levels of the starve cycle.

> *Certain types of massage release endorphins into your bloodstream and lower your levels of the stress hormone, cortisol.*

Other applications for massage have included its use during childbirth and labour to reduce pain. Although these researchers have not assessed its effects on women's stress levels, another study looked at both stress and pain in children who were suffering from rheumatoid arthritis. Nightly massage of the limbs of these children not only relieved their pain but also decreased their anxiety levels.

Sunlight

> *Goodness comes out of people who bask in the*
> *sun as it does out of a sweet apple roasted before the fire.*
> CHARLES DUDLEY WARNER

Most psychologists say that there are two boom times in their practices. The first is straight after Christmas when everyone has been fighting the family for an extended period; the problems then are to do with relationships. The second is in midwinter, and the problem then is depression.

Darkness and the blues

Have you ever suffered from the 'midwinter blues'? Have you ever wondered about the effects of living in a country where it is dark most of the day in winter? In Scandinavia, where there is only about one hour's daylight in midwinter, the winter suicide rate is the highest in the world. It's true that most of us do feel happier and more positive in the summer than in the winter, and there may be a biochemical reason for this.

Seasonal Affective Disorder

Since the 1980s there has been growing interest in a condition known as Seasonal Affective Disorder or SAD. Sufferers complain of depression in the winter and weight gain, combined with low energy and cravings for carbohydrate-rich foods. They go to sleep early and stay in bed for nine or 10 hours. This is different from ordinary depression, which is generally accompanied by insomnia. But people with SAD complain that their sleep is light and not fully refreshing. They say they often feel drowsy in the day and have trouble concentrating. When spring comes the depression goes. SAD has been found to affect both children and adults.

SAD is particularly common at high latitudes in both the northern and southern hemispheres. One study estimated that it is 16 times more common in the northern regions of the United States, in states like Minnesota and Maine, than in the southern states like Florida and Texas.

Researchers are not entirely clear what the chemical cause of SAD is and in fact there may be more than one cause. It may have something to do with a neurotransmitter called melatonin that the brain secretes during the dark. Light suppresses the secretion of melatonin. Various theories have been tested. Perhaps people who have SAD secrete too much melatonin or secrete it for too long or secrete it at the wrong time of the day. SAD may also have something to do with the chemical serotonin, which plays a major role in depression. Some studies have shown low serotonin levels in those with SAD and an increase in serotonin after exposure to bright light.

Other researchers have surmised that SAD may be caused by seasonal changes in the brain's thyroid hormones. Some of the symptoms of SAD, such as low energy and weight gain, are also found in people with an underactive thyroid gland. We do know, however, that exposing SAD sufferers to bright light can eliminate the depression and tiredness as well as the craving for carbohydrates.

Light therapy

Light therapy is not new. As far back as 1910 a Dr J. H. Kellogg of Michigan, USA, was treating patients with various forms of light therapy for what he called melancholia, the depression of today. His methods were not supported by research and the study of light therapy was dropped until the early 1980s. Researchers in Europe and America are now trying what they call photo therapy with depressed patients. They expose their patients to rooms that are intensely lit with lights approximating the brightness of the sun. The unit we use to measure light's brightness is called the lux. Normal indoor lights have a brightness of 250–500 lux. Sunlight ranges from 10,000 lux on a cloudy day to 80,000 on a clear day near the equator. To be effective in combating SAD the light needs to be at least 2500 lux. The length of time patients spend in bright light has ranged from two to six hours a day. The time of day the treatment is given does have an effect: evening treatment has been shown to be less effective.

There seems good evidence that photo therapy works if you suffer from SAD or winter depression, and some evidence that it may work if you suffer from depression at any other time of the year too.

Researchers in California compared two groups of depressed war veterans. These were not SAD sufferers; they had been depressed a long time. One group was given three hours of bright light a day; the other was given three hours of dim red light. The veterans themselves thought that the red light would help them more, but after a week the groups who received the bright light not only said they felt less depressed than before, but their scores on pencil and paper tests of depression had improved. Their improvement was significantly greater than the group exposed to red light.

Boost your sun intake: banish the blues

The lives many of us live today decrease the amount of time we spend in the sun. Trapped in indoor jobs in artificially lit workplaces, we are exposed to far less sunlight than our ancestors were. One study in San Diego looked at the amount of time healthy elderly people spent in the sun. Men spent on average 75 minutes a day, women 20 minutes. If you're working full-time you probably get even less sunlight than this.

What can you do to ensure you get more sunlight? Don't hibernate in your house in the winter; go out on bright days. Make sure your house is a sunny one if you can. If it's not, and you can put skylights in, do. If you can afford to, take a holiday in the sun in winter.

Laughter

Cheerfulness sir is the principal ingredient in the composition of health.
ARTHUR MURPHY

Much of the evidence on the role of laughter as an antidote to stress is anecdotal; you certainly do feel better if you've had a good laugh or you've been to a funny movie.

Laugh and live longer

A team of medical researchers in Maryland, USA found that people with heart disease were 40 percent less likely to laugh in humorous situations than those with healthy hearts. The people with heart disease were much less likely even to recognise humour and generally displayed more anger and hostility than those who were well.

Laughter is much more than moving your muscles and making a noise. We now know that when you laugh a variety of hormones and chemicals are released into your bloodstream. Some of these are the same as those released during the stress response; in fact, some researchers regard laughter as a form of stress, calling it eustress or good stress.

> *When you laugh a variety of hormones and chemicals are released into your bloodstream.*

Investigators in California have shown that when you laugh, an entirely different pattern of hormones and chemicals enters the bloodstream compared with when you're emotionally upset or not stressed at all. They showed a group of subjects a 60 minute humour videotape, put catheters in their arms to collect their blood and took blood samples every 10 minutes to see what chemicals were released during the time they were watching the film. They compared these blood samples with blood from a control group of volunteers who merely sat around quietly for the same length of time.

The control group's chemical levels remained stable over the course of the study. But the group who watched the funny video showed both a reduction in two of the important stress chemicals dopac and cortisol, and also in adrenaline.

The researchers concluded that laughter is able to lower stress: when you laugh there are fewer of the harmful stress chemicals in your bloodstream than there are when you're simply relaxed, and you feel better emotionally. Laughter is a positive emotion and it improves the quality of your life.

They also suggested that laughter can boost your immune system, because cortisol and adrenaline are both chemicals which destroy the cells of your immune system. Other studies by this same group have shown that laughter increases the rate at which your immune cells reproduce themselves and the rate at which they destroy foreign invader cells.

> *Laughter is able to lower stress and boost the immune system.*

What tickles your funny bone?

Decide what makes you laugh. Is it movies or plays, TV comedy shows or books, or is it particular people whose sense of humour you appreciate? Plan how you can put these into your life, not occasionally but frequently. Don't watch only the dramas and the documentaries on television, watch the comedies too. Don't read only books of fact or serious fiction, keep a book of humour on the go all the time. If you have friends who make you laugh, see them regularly.

Putting it all together

As far back as 1956 Hans Selye said that 'What we need is a stress reduction technique that involves daily ways of looking at and interacting with others.' He felt specifically that we need to do things each day that involve the creation of feelings of accomplishment and security in ourselves by inspiring in others love, goodwill and gratitude for what we have done or what we are likely to do in the future.

Altruism and unselfishness are probably important factors in helping you to live a less stressful life, but perhaps the real gem in Selye's words is the emphasis on a daily reduction in stress and the creation of positive feelings. Don't just put the Five Step Life Plan into action when your life starts going wrong for you. Make it a daily part of the way you live your life:

• Your attitude to life is positive and optimistic.
• You believe your problems are solvable or not worth killing yourself over.

- You make sure your biochemistry is in balance.
- You regularly keep fit, eat and sleep well and spend time in the sun.
- You make sure you are doing what you value and you have lots in your life you enjoy and look forward to.

If you do these things, you will find that it takes very little to make you laugh, and that fun comes easily. You will also have the peace of mind that comes with a firm hand on the reins of your life and a gilt edged insurance policy against stress in the future.

Your Life Plan: Step 5

1. List the things that are of value to you in your life. Arrange them in order of priority and then examine your life to see whether it reflects those priorities. If your family is your major priority, for example, are you giving it due attention and place in your life?
2. Plan your weeks and plan your years. Decide on any goals you want to achieve in line with your priorities. Consider your personal goals also.
3. List all the activities that you enjoy, both the large and the small. Make sure that you have enough of them in your life so that you have things to look forward to. Schedule them into your day, your week and your year. Dwell on the positive events in your life.
4. Decide whether you have enough periods of peace in your life. Are you getting enough sleep? Do you need to put massage into your week? Have you enough free time in the weekends or at the end of your work projects? Are you taking time out with holidays?
5. Is your diet adequate?
6. Are you getting out in the sun enough, particularly in the winter? Do you need to take up some activity that will take you outside more often? Is your house sunny enough?
7. Are you getting enough fun and laughter? You can do this with movies, plays and television shows, you can do it with books, you can do it by spending time with people who make you happy.

Paul's Life Plan: Step 5

My values

Once my head was clear and my thoughts were less negative, I felt my back wasn't against the wall anymore. I started to look at my life, instead of being in crisis mode, fending off the problems as they were flying at me. I looked at what was important to me and I asked myself whether my life of the last few years really reflected those values. It didn't. Becky and the kids meant more to me than anything else and yet if I looked at the amount of time I'd spent with them – particularly with the kids – it was minuscule compared with the time I'd spent at work.

My father was more important to me than my work too, and yet I'd virtually ignored him over the past six months.

I decided right then that this would have to change – no more working till 9 or 10 at night, I would try to leave work at six. Even if I had to work late, I'd come home for dinner with Becky and the kids and go back afterwards. I also made a vow that I would ask Dad over at least once a week for a meal, and that Becky and the kids and I would take a holiday as soon as I came back from Boston.

Laughter

I was always someone who found it hard to laugh out loud, even if I thought something was funny, so I decided I needed to laugh more. Now, about once a fortnight Becky and I rent a comedy video. At first I used to watch them with a sort of suppressed smile on my face, but now I roar with laughter. And it's infectious. Becky laughs too. Laughter really has been terrific therapy for me.

Enjoyment

I did another thing that sounds small, but it's part of being a different, revitalised Paul. I asked Becky if she could recommend an action I could take that was new for me; something that would reinforce the idea that I was a good person. She said, 'Remember people's birthdays. Men never do. Go through your desk diary and write down the birthdays of all of our friends. And call them on their birthday. It's just another way of connecting.' And so I have. Even with guys I know quite well, they sound taken aback when you call and say, 'Hi Nick, happy birthday'. But it always leads to a conversation and you tell by the tone of their voice that they're pleased. And afterwards I'm always glad I rang.

My trip to Boston ended up feeling, in one way, like an anticlimax. I delivered the report and answered some hard questions about the company, but nobody took me to task personally. I couldn't believe I had ever been so tortured by the prospect of it. I used the thought-stopping and I know I came across as calm and on top of it. I didn't have to use it all that much; I'd just become a more laid-back person. I even looked a different person, my face was relaxed and able to smile again. I actually had a good time in Boston. My American colleagues took me around town in the evenings after work and I made a good impression.

I've been consciously managing my stress for about six months now. I still find thought-stopping the most effective technique for fast attitude adjustment, but I need to use it less and less. I no longer feel depressed. I'm in good shape physically because of the exercise and good shape mentally because I now tell Becky what's on my mind instead of expecting her to be some kind of psychic. I don't expect her to come to my rescue. I feel confident that I can handle things myself. I've had to be vigilant with myself in focusing on the positives in my day. It hasn't been automatic. When people say, 'Hi Paul, how are you?', part of me still wants to say grudgingly, 'Oh, I'm okay.' But I resist that now. I say, 'I feel really good. How are you?', and the moment I've done that, I actually do feel really good.

Before, when I had some intractable problem at work I would bend over backwards, working all kinds of ridiculous hours in a state of high anxiety trying to fix it, even when I knew that I couldn't. I used to think if I just suffered enough over it, somehow I wouldn't be blamed. Now I keep in my mind that there are some things you can't change. Sometimes mistakes happen and you have to own up to them and move on.

Like everyone, I still have days when I want to murder my fellow motorists or I'm swearing at the mower because it won't start, but it's a moment of ill temper that passes. It doesn't characterise my life. And I apologise to people if I'm out of line. Sometimes I wake up in the morning and it can be raining and I remember I forgot to put the garbage out and I've got a tough 8.30 a.m. meeting coming up, but I can still say to myself, 'I'm happy to be alive.' And I mean it.

Index